AF174137

PRAISE FOR *NOIRYORICAN*

"With considerable style, poise, and humor, Richie Narvaez's *Noiryorican* unpacks a world of grifters, street punks and hangers-on just trying to get by in the big city when the odds are stacked against them. At his street poet best Narvaez gives Jonathan Lethem and Junot Diaz a run for their money. I loved this collection."

—Adrian McKinty, bestselling author of *The Chain*

"In this eclectic collection of noir stories, Narvaez takes the reader across the boroughs of New York City, Puerto Rico, LA, and Texas. Open this book and take this ride through the mazes of Narvaez's imagination."

—Ivelisse Rodriguez, author of *Love War Stories*

NOIRYORICAN

BOOKS BY RICHIE NARVAEZ

Hipster Death Rattle
Holly Hernandez and the Death of Disco
Roachkiller and Other Stories
Noiryorican

RICHIE NARVAEZ

NOIRYORICAN

Collection Copyright © 2020 by Richie Narvaez

"The Godfather of Williamsburg" is new to this collection; all other stories have been previously published.

All rights reserved. No part of the book may be reproduced in any form or by any electronic or mechanical means, including information storage and retrieval systems, without permission in writing from the publisher, except by a reviewer who may quote brief passages in a review.

Down & Out Books
3959 Van Dyke Road, Suite 265
Lutz, FL 33558
DownAndOutBooks.com

The characters and events in this book are fictitious. Any similarity to real persons, living or dead, is coincidental and not intended by the author.

Cover design by Zach McCain

ISBN: 1-64396-120-9
ISBN-13: 978-1-64396-120-0

This is for my Aunt Terry,
who showed me the way to escape

TABLE OF CONTENTS

INTRODUCTION

Why not write about nice people?

The truth is I'm not very interested in nice people, at least not when it comes to writing. I like having beers with people who call their mothers every Sunday and who recycle, but I'd rather write about contract killers, con men, and crooked cops. And for my subgenre of choice here—noir—there are few if any nice people. As Megan Abbott has noted, "In noir, everyone is fallen."

Now, "noir" is one of those labels that gets misused a lot, like "organic," "gluten-free," and "great." Too many readers see "noir" and picture private eyes and femme fatales bantering in offices dim with carcinogens. But that's hard-boiled fiction, errant knights and damsels in distress, fine stuff, but more film noir than literary noir or roman noir.

I like to think of "noir" the way Charles Ardai does: "Noir depicts lives beset by disappointment, frustration and cruelty, in a universe that is indifferent at best and malign at worst."

In other words, you won't find any happy endings in this volume.

At the same time, these stories in this book heavily feature Puerto Rican or Latino/a/x/e characters, people you don't see much of in crime fiction or in most popular fiction at all. I

1

thought it was important to give characters who come from the same background as I do, who often end up as little more than background, starring roles at the front of the stage. Oh, FYI:

NOIRYORICAN = NOIR + NUYORICAN
(New York-born Puerto Rican)

In case you were wondering.

You might also wonder: Why take a group of people who so often and so cruelly get maligned as criminals and associate them in any way with crime? Well, every other group has their crime fiction, everyone else has their shot at a piece of the pop culture pie, why not us? Latina/o/x/e people are of course as complex as anyone else. Many of the people in these stories are broken, depressed, desperate. They make really, really bad decisions. You've made a few of those, haven't you? And sometimes you might find them laughable or pathetic. But that doesn't mean the journeys they take are any less compelling, instructive, or human than your own.

As to the stories themselves:

"Good Fences" is one of several flash fiction pieces sprinkled throughout the book. It was originally written for a zine I used to publish called *Zeeno*. Get it? Moving on. This story was also one of the first crime fiction tales I ever wrote, and it is based on story told to me that is either true or a very bizarre lie. Two tough-guy cops who happen to be neighbors have an unneighborly encounter incited by dogs leaping over a fence.

"The Godfather of Williamsburg" is a prequel to the story "Roachkiller," which was published by *Murdaland,* one of a wave of literary crime fic magazines from early this century. That story was an also-ran in *The Best American Mystery Stories of 2008,* and it opened the door for me to several anthologies. People have often asked about the hitman protagonist, who has an unusual habit of referring to himself in third person, so I invited him back. This story, which appears here for the first time, is based on a real-life kidnapping that took place in Brooklyn in 1979 and involved the numbers runner my father worked for back then. Which is a tale for another time.

I have great memories of going to Orchard Beach as a kid. Eating bologna sandwiches and cold fried chicken from the cooler, running from the heat into the greenish water. It's a man-made beach, shaped like a crescent, and tucked up high in the Bronx. Because of its popularity with my people in the '60s and '70s, it became known as the Puerto Rican Riviera. I went back a few years ago and was upset at how the architecture had been left to decay. There are frequent calls to revive the area, but the Bronx is still waiting. That visit inspired the story "Merry Xmas from Orchard Beach." I liked the idea of juxtaposing a non-beach holiday onto a beach setting, and then Heather Rincon's charmingly abrasive voice popped into my head.

Another flash fiction story drafted during my zine days, "Withhold the Dawn" was originally written in script form as a parody of an old-fashioned crime radio melodrama. I read about the call for "flash noir" for the anthology *Tiny Crimes: Very Short Tales of Mystery and Murder,* and I dug up this old story and revised it heavily. I wrote it with full freak flag flying, and, even though I tweaked its form, it retains much of my unadulterated, unadult humor, such as it is. Sincere apologies to Don McLean.

Written for an anthology called *Grand Central Noir*—and just that title is a fantastic setup—"Meet Me at the Clock" is another story built from setting. I had only an inkling of what to write. Then I took a trip to the bustling Beaux-Arts commuter hellhole, and in exploring its beauty and its bowels, I found Platform 13, an isolated area that looks like it's been abandoned since WWII. That gave me the idea to make the protagonist a man in the wrong time, and it gave me a perfect spot to set the climax.

Nordic noir, that blue-tinted, breath-frosted, emotionally muted crime fiction of frozen territories, had become extremely popular in the 2000s, threatening to overtake the noiriness of warmer climates, where most roman noir had been set since the '50s. My dear friend Annamaria Alfieri invited me to contribute to an anthology she and author Michael Stanley were putting together called *Sunshine Noir*. They wanted to swing the focus of noir back to where the mercury climbs. For this story, I took a (mental) trip back to Puerto Rico and read up on recent events. The island has been struggling for a long while under a recession, massive debt, and corruption. Then I found the story of a floundering Puerto Rico golf club/resort that a certain billionaire was supposed to save. That was the spark for "Pale Yellow Sun."

I met Ehsan Ehsani, the mind behind *Mystery Tribune,* when he came to a Mystery Writers of America meeting just after he'd launched his literary crime fiction magazine, and he was looking to meet people in the community. I introduced him around as best I could, I think he bought me a drink, and we've been friends ever since (not just because of the drink), hanging out at all the crime fiction fêtes in town. I'd done some articles for him, but for years I struggled for the right fiction piece to send to *MT*. This was it. Many readers believe a noir story must involve a private investigator, but that's not even true in film noir. But here, just for them, is a private eye story. "Blackout" comes with a heavy pour of schadenfreude, one of the chief ingredients of noir.

The online journal *Shotgun Honey* publishes short, sharp flash fiction, 700 words tops, no exceptions. This story was written expressly for them and is a parody of "How to Date a Brown Girl (Black Girl, White Girl, or Halfie)" by Junot Diaz. Once I studied the voice and came up with the premise, "How To Kill A Brown Girl (Or Black, White, Or Halfsie)" came together—if not in a flash, at least within a week.

Cannibalism and noir: two great tastes that taste great together. Dana C. Kabel, another author I met through the New York City crime-writer scene, asked me to contribute to his anthology *Skin & Bones*. It features a menu of stories by the likes of Lawrence Block, Tess Makovesky, Stuart Neville, just to namedrop a few, so I'm glad I was lucky enough to, er, make the cut. In most cannibal stories, the element of anthropophagy appears as a twist. But in "Black Friday," I started out tongue in cheek. Sorry. Useless trivia note: The surname "Arens" is a reference to a professor-mentor of mine at Stony Brook who wrote the book *The Man-Eating Myth,* which hypothesized that cannibalism was never a socially accepted practice and that calling a group of people "cannibals" was particularly insidious kind of Othering.

Author Angel Luis Colon emailed me in 2018 and said he was putting together a noir anthology called *¡Pa'que Tu Lo Sepas! Stories to Benefit the People of Puerto* Rico and that the profits would go to help people affected by the disaster of Hurricane Maria. I volunteered a story immediately. Of course then I had to write it. For inspiration, I turned to the folk legend Juan Bobo from the island and for form, well, I had always wanted to do my version of Ring Lardner's "Haircut." The unreliable narrator in "Bobo" speaks in my head just like my uncle Jose.

As a writer I believe one should not live by one genre alone. For the sake of variety, here's a horror story for you. But don't worry, crime fiction fans, it has violence and death. You might sum up "Old Pendejo" as *Old Yeller* meets *Night of the Living Dead.* FYI: "pendejos" is Spanish for "short hairs," and you can figure out where on the body these are located. But to call someone a "pendejo" is slang, meaning that person is an "idiot" or "pain in the neck." Add the word to your vocabulary to entertain friends at parties.

I grew up on a steady diet of *Justice League, Batman, The Incredible Hulk, Deathlok, The Demon,* on and on. Comic books and superheroes were my bible and my Jesuses. So of course I've always wanted to write superhero stories, and I did do some freelance work for DC Comics in the '90s, mostly children's book stuff, coloring books, all for hire and not my own creations.

5

So when I found out about *A Thousand Faces,* a literary journal that published superhero stories, I immediately put on my Green Lantern ring, started typing, and out flew "La Volcana."

The final story, "Southside Valentine," is not noir, but I thought you might need respite from all the tragic endings. It's a flash story, which developed from the title, two words that popped into my head and that I was determined to make a story out of. This once again takes place in my old neighborhood, my favorite writing ground, Williamsburg, Brooklyn.

Richie Narvaez
Bronx, New York
January 2020

GOOD FENCES

Jose walked out his front door on Metropolitan Avenue, down the stoop, and over to his neighbor Frank's door. He rang the bell twice.

"I want to talk to you about your dogs," Jose said.

Frank was sixty-eight, a retired cop, just like Jose. Well over six feet tall, Frank stood behind the barely opened door and blocked any view of the inside. His bushy eyebrows didn't move. His big, dried fig of a face stayed blank. He said, "Yeah?"

"They bark all day. They never stop barking. Then they do their business right there by the fence. You can smell it. It brings flies."

Frank said, "What do you want me to do about it? They're dogs. They gotta do what they gotta do."

"But they never stop barking."

"Cheapest burglar alarm known to man," Frank said, sipping from the beer can in his hand.

"So we got burglars trying to break in all day long?" Jose said, trying to be funny.

Frank didn't laugh.

Through his thirty-five years on the force, of seeing the dark things that people could do to each other, Jose had kept up his optimism, his hope. He thought people were essentially good eggs.

7

"Listen," he said, "could you chain 'em up, at least? They jump the fence sometimes. Do me that favor, will ya? I would sure appreciate it."

"Righto," Frank said. "Don't you worry."

Just that Labor Day, a few weeks before, Jose's daughter had visited and told him to get out more. "Don't just sit here in your own stink," she'd said. "Use the backyard." He told her about the dogs. "It's your backyard, Pop. Screw the dogs." So, trying his best to ignore the barking and the smell, he started up his old grill. He got out two two-pound burgers seasoned just the way his wife used to like it, garlic powder, lots of pepper. The phone had rung. He went inside to answer it. When he came back, he saw the butcher's paper in the middle of the yard, shiny, empty. Over the short fence, the dogs, for once, were not barking. They licked their lips, looking at Jose to see what else he had to offer.

A month after the talk on the stoop, Jose looked over the fence into his neighbor's yard. The two dogs—mutts with a lot of German Shepherd blood—were connected on a long, thick chain, chained to each other but nothing else.

And still they barked. And still the smell, still the flies.

Frank had gotten the dogs to keep him company after his wife had divorced him and hotfooted it to Kissimmee. He had marched the mutts through the house and into the backyard, and they never went inside again. He had taken one of the doors off his old plastic shed and let them sleep in there. He liked to sit in his kitchen and watch them. He liked watching the dogs dig up and shit on anything that was left of his ex-wife's flower garden.

Soon after he got the chains for the dogs, Frank came back from a long walk around the neighborhood—what he liked to think of as his beat—and saw a brand-new, six-foot tall fence between his side and his neighbor Jose's.

"Son of bitch," Frank said.

Jose had splurged, spending more money than he could afford. Years ago, it had been fun to be neighbors with another fellow on the job, have parties, drinks. But really it had been their wives who were friends, never the men. Jose loved the new fence with its faux grass weave. It made him feel like he was in a forest. The dogs kept up the barking but now Jose didn't have to see them—or smell them—as much. He would do some planting this week, but today he would finally sit out in his own backyard with the paper.

First he made himself iced tea and a bologna sandwich. Then he remembered the lawn chair was in the basement. So he went downstairs to get it, and, look at that, there was a picture of his beautiful Cecilia on top of a box, one of the many he still had to go through and clean out like his daughter had been nagging him to do. So he found the lawn chair, opened it, and got one of the boxes, and under one of his wife's old hats—it still smelled like her perfume—under it he found an envelope full of photographs. Cecilia at a party. Cecilia at a restaurant. He didn't recognize any of the places. And then there was Cecilia with two men. Neither of which was him. A hotel room, it looked like. They were all naked. He recognized one of the men, the guy with the dried fig face. Tears fogged Jose's thick glasses.

Meanwhile, over at Frank's, the dogs barked, louder than ever, feral, rasping barks. Two six packs in, Frank shut the blinds and cranked up the radio and took a nap. The alcohol in his system woke him up only a little while later. In the john, he realized something was missing and then he realized what it was: he couldn't hear his dogs.

"Son of a bitch," he said.

Frank went out the back door and then saw something that surprised him, even after all the horror he had seen on the force. One dog hung over his side of the fence, tongue bloated, sticking way out. He walked to the fence and stood on a cinder block to look over. Sure enough, on the other end of the chain, the other dog hung down, tongue bloated, sticking way out.

The dogs hung in perfect harmony, necks snapped perfectly.

One must have jumped the fence. The other had tried, maybe

an instant behind the other, an instant too late. Goddamn dogs. Frank began to shake. What the hell did they want to go and jump the fence for?

He stood on the cinderblock again, over at his neighbor Jose's side and saw a fatty, blood-red lamb shank on an unwrapped piece of butcher's paper in the middle of the yard.

"Son of a bitch," he said. "Son of a bitch."

Tears stinging his eyes, cursing his stupid damn dogs, Frank got out a .22 he'd picked up at a crime scene he forgot how many years ago, serial numbers filed off. He loaded it. Then he walked out his front door on Metropolitan Avenue, down the stoop, and over to Joe's door, and then he rang the bell twice.

Jose was sitting on the couch watching TV when he heard the bell. He got up and went to answer it with a double-barreled shotgun.

THE GODFATHER OF WILLIAMSBURG

Roachkiller wasn't always the Roachkiller Roachkiller is today. It took time. See what I'm saying.

Turn back that clock.

Back in the day, eighteen years old, dressed in Roachkiller's best polyester seamless pants, polyester shirt, and of course razor-thin-tipped roachkiller boots—Roachkiller's patriotic red, white, and blue pair—because it was July 4th and that was how you did it. But where was Roachkiller? Out on the block smoking a doobie to celebrate liberty? Out at Coney Island catching rays with the sweetest squeeze in the world—at that time—Miriam?

Naw, man.

Roachkiller was down in the hot-as-ass basement of the punk-ass Pizza Palace with his jive-ass uncle, Tio Cheo, surrounded by the rotten smell of live rooster, rooster shit, dried-up beer, and dead rat. Floor to ceiling a mess of wooden cages, each with a nasty-smelling bird sticking its head out looking at the humans.

"You take Rocky," Tio Cheo said, opening a cage, handing over a big-ass red rooster. "I'll take Apollo."

The city had been cracking down on the cockfighting circuit, so all the games was closing down. But what do you do with dozens of retired roosters? The same thing you do with any evidence. You get rid of it.

"Go ahead," Tio said, then he demonstrated, taking the rooster he had in his hand, stretching its neck with two hands, the motherfucking bird flapping its wings, screaming squawking, *Kuh-kuh-kuh-kuh-KACK!* And once that shit started, all the other roosters in their cages started doing the same thing. Then Apollo stopped moving and Tio threw it on the floor.

"These are going to get cooked up for some *asopao de pollo,* but they're tough bastards, so you gotta cook them all day before you can eat them." He went to another cage, grabbed another one, killed it, threw it on the floor. "Make sure to take one for your grandmother. I promised her."

But Tio saw that Roachkiller still had his bird in his hand. Roachkiller tried, but with every stretch that tough bastard Rocky looked at Roachkiller with those tiny, blinking eyes. Accusing me. Begging me.

"C'mon," Tio said. "Don't be a latrine-green recruit. It's not like you don't know what choking the chicken is like. Hahaha." He was an ex-marine with chest and arms like Chinese Hercules. He had a small dark hole in his right eyelid he said came from a bullet, and he liked to say he was able to survive Vietnam because he could keep an eye on the enemy even while he was asleep.

Roachkiller held the rooster up to him and, with one good twist, the thing was dead.

Tio smiled. "See? Easy! C'mon. Next one."

The next one was easy, the one after that easier. It don't take as long as you'd think, taking the life out of things. It don't take so long at all, once you get the hang of it.

At the end there was a pile of dead roosters. No more tiny eyes blinking at you.

"Look at your hands," Tio Cheo said, laughing. "That's how it starts."

12

Blood and feathers and slime covered Roachkiller's hands. There was a closet-size bathroom with a bare bulb, no toilet seat, no running water.

"Fuck!" There was even shit on Roachkiller's boots. "Tio! Look at this!"

A woman came down the narrow stairs with a laundry bag and started tossing the dead roosters into it. Tio Cheo held one for himself and held up another for Roachkiller when some fat guy came squeezing down the stairs and said, "Cheo! I heard you was down here."

"Guiso! Is Benny upstairs? I brought my nephew to meet him."

"You didn't hear what happened?"

"No. What happened?"

"Benny's at the house. You better go right away."

"I'll take him a rooster."

"Leave the rooster. Go right away."

In Tio Cheo's Chevy Lacuna, speeding down Bushwick Avenue, all garages, bodegas, and jean stores back then, Tio said, "You know why I picked you up today?"

Roachkiller was still trying to get shit off his shoes. "To kill chickens."

"Naw, boy, that was just practice. I had to see how strong you were. C'mon, why?"

"Because you don't want Roachkiller to have no fun."

"You know, why do you keep talking that way? It makes no sense. Just be Roberto, man. That's your father's name. It's your name. Just use it, be proud of it."

Roachkiller thought he was all growed up by then. Though he wasn't too far from Saturday morning cartoon, Malta India, Yoo-Hoo, Tip Top, cherry red *piragua* melting down his arm. But Roachkiller had hair on his balls and no one could tell him shit. So he played with the 8-track of Fania All-Stars, jumping from track to track, tried to ignore Tio.

"I picked you up today because I got a job for you," Tio said.

"It's the 4th of July. Nobody works 4th of July."

"Bullshit. The men who work, they always work. There ain't no days off. Not even Christmas. Listen, your mother's been talking to me and she's worried because you dropped out of high school way back, you don't have a job and it don't look like you want a job."

"You got that right."

Roachkiller was making fine money. Sometimes there was a car or TV store to boost, but better was hooking people up at the disco because then the disco was the place for fun and the place for business. Who needed anything else?

"The good thing is you ain't got nobody pregnant yet, far as we know." Tio knocked on the dashboard. "But you can't spend all your nights out at the clubs with no future. You gotta have a trade. So that's what I'm doing. I'm helping you out and taking you to meet Benny. You met him before, at your father's funeral. You probably don't remember."

"Roachkiller remembers him."

Benny Alicea was the big collector for the numbers racket in Williamsburg, covering everything from the Navy Yard up to Grand Street and over to Flushing Avenue. Every bet in the neighborhood, from a nickel to a thousand bucks, had to go through him.

"I'm introducing you now as a man. And now you gotta talk to him with respect. You know we call him the Godfather now. At first, it was like a joke, when the movie came out. You know the movie?"

"Everybody knows the movie!"

"Benny's been around a long time now, and he's built up a crew, and he's always looking for new recruits. And it sounds like he might be having some trouble, so this'll be a good opportunity for you. See what I'm saying?"

Tio Cheo drove to East New York and slowed the car down in front of a house on Jerome Avenue, across the street from a schoolyard. There were a bunch of police cars parked in front.

"Stay cool," Tio said to himself more than to Roachkiller, and he pulled past the cops and found a spot around the corner. Two men were standing there, and one Roachkiller recognized as Johnny D. walked up to the car.

"Cheo. Get inside." He was a serious guy, brown and hard like a brick, wearing shades and a black-and-purple guayabera that looked like it had just come off the ironing board.

"What's up with the cops?"

"Don't worry. Just say you're a friend of the family, if they ask."

"What's going on?"

"They kidnapped Benny's wife and daughter last night."

"Holy shit."

"Go inside. He's been asking for you."

There were cops up and down the sidewalk like a gauntlet, but Roachkiller and Tio Cheo walked cool as Bomb Pops into the house, door wide open.

Right inside the gated door was the living room. Benny sat in the middle of a plastic-covered red coach. He wore a white polyester guayabera, white pants, black ankle boots. He had a mustache black and thick as a belt on a take-no-shit face, and he nodded at us as we all walked in.

Standing over him was a cop in a black suit with a yellow tie, sweatstains on his collar. "Seventy-five grand," the cop was saying. "You want to tell me how these kidnappers think you have that kind of cash? Help me understand that, Mr. Alicea."

Benny leaned forward, smooth shouldered, *cara palo*. He was surrounded by cops who probably wanted to beat his ass but you could see Benny was the one in control. "I be honest," he said. "I got no idea. Like I told you, I'm just a simple tobacco seller. I make two-seventy-five a week. These are criminals. I don't know what they are thinking."

15

The cop in the stained shirt said, "Maybe because you drive that brand-new Buick parked outside."

"It is brand new, sure, but I got a good deal on it. If you want the name of the dealer, I get it for you."

"No gracias, *amigo*. You said they took the money you had on you? How much was that?"

"About eight hundred dollars, more or less."

"That's a hell of a lot of tobacco, Mr. Alicea."

"I had just took it out the bank because we're supposed to go on a family vacation. And it wasn't enough for these guys. They got greedy. They must think I got money coming out of my ass."

"Maybe you do, since you've set yourself up as the local big shot and go around calling yourself 'Godfather.' A spic Godfather, of all the fucking things. Who'da thought?"

Another cop came over and pulled the first one away.

Benny relaxed back into the plastic-covered couch with a crunch. Roachkiller could see easy what he was doing was all fake. The cop could probably see it, too. But it didn't seem like anybody cared.

Johnny D. came in and led Tio and Roachkiller down a long hall and to a kitchen. No cops there. He pointed to the table, which was covered with *comida criolla* takeout.

"Who's this?" he said, looking Roachkiller up and down.

"My nephew, Rob—"

"Roachkiller."

"Roachkiller? Like those shoes?"

Johnny D. looked down at Roachkiller's supersharp, supersexy, superpointed boots. Clean now. "You could stab somebody with those," he said.

"Yeah. So?" said Roachkiller.

"This one has balls, Cheo."

"Like boulders," Cheo said.

"Sit down here, kid. Eat. You're family. This house is your house."

16

Roachkiller was shameless hungry, so he sat down and started chowing down on the *arroz con pollo* and the pile of *platanos* laid out.

Johnny D. sat at the table and whispered to us. "Last night Benny was going to the Pizza Palace II, the one on Myrtle. He gets out of the car and some young thing—you know how Benny likes them young—she starts flirting with him and whatnot. All of a sudden, four guys pop out of nowhere, put him back in his car and make him drive home. They took all the money he had in the house but they wanted more. He told them he didn't have it, so they instead took Ada and Lydia."

"Ada's his wife," Tio said to me. "Lydia's his daughter. She's thirteen."

"Fourteen. Another thing," Johnny D. said. "Those are G-Men in there, not just cops. They all showed up this morning out of nowhere. How they found out about this we don't know. But first the kidnappers wanted ten grand. The Feds show, and now they want seventy-five. The Feds are going to stick to Benny like glue for a while. So here's what he wants. You gotta find out who did this before the Feds do."

"Copy that." Tio practically saluted the guy. "We're on it."

"And how we supposed to find these guys?" Roachkiller said.

"I was special ops in Vietnam," Tio said. "I have ways."

"Listen to your uncle, kid. Now eat fast and get your asses out of here."

"Roachkiller don't want no part of this. Roachkiller stays under the radar. No Feds on me."

In the Lacuna on the way back, Tio Cheo kept his eyes on the road, but Roachkiller could swear he was looking at him through the hole in his eyelid, looking at him hard-hearted as a nun.

"Boy, we've been assigned a mission and we ain't going to fail."

17

"Nah, man, count Roachkiller out."

"You're talking like you got a choice, *sobrino*. You owe me, and you owe your family. Why do you think your ma and abuela are not on the *gwelfare*? Who do you think has been supporting your family since your father died, huh? You think your grandmother and mother cleaning houses is enough to take care of you and your big fat brother? You know I been paying your rent, paying electricity, gas, paying for groceries?"

"You remind us every day."

"You bet I do, you spoiled brat. You know what your problem is?"

"No, but you're gonna tell Roachkiller."

"You problem is you grew up here, not back in the old country, not back on the island. You don't know how tough life can be, shitting in a hole in the ground, not having meat for days. You got no idea. You had it easy. You're spoiled rotten. Your grandmother and mother give you way too much and you give them nothing. Probably why you talk so weird, all about yourself all the time, plus all that sugar they put in the breakfast cereal."

"But Ro—. But I give Abuela money."

"Chump change. You spend most of your money on fancy shoes and dime bags that you sell to the fags and the Jews at them discos. Yeah, I know about your part-time work. You can't get shit past me. I used to do special ops in Vietnam. I have—"

Enough of this bullshit. Tio Cheo was slowing down at the light, and Roachkiller saw his chance—"I'm outta here, man"—opening the door, and running in boots down the block and up the stairs to the elevated train at Hewes Street.

Roachkiller took the train deeper into Brooklyn, back to Miriam's crib on Central Avenue to chill. Knocked three times on the door and before she could get "What the heck are you doin' here?" out of her sweet mouth, Roachkiller's lips were on hers, and she was "Mmmmming" backwards to her bedroom where the plaster statue of St. Jude looked down from the wardrobe, rocking and rocking and always about to fall off but never quite.

Roachkiller had a baby face back then but he had pull to get into any disco in the city. Paradise Garage, Studio 54, Le Clique, Roseland Ballroom, Bond's. Back in the day, Roachkiller went to all of them and had special friends at each one. Special friends meaning customers.

At Bond's that night, everyone was getting down, DJ mixing into Cerrone, dancers doing their thing, Roachkiller spinning Miriam around and going in for a kiss—when he spied a short dude trying to get his attention, pointing to a hallway with his head. Dude was goofy and nervous about it, uncool.

"Be right back, baby."

"Where you goin'?" Miriam said. "I was just getting warmed up." She was one of the high-yellow, moon-faced Puerto Rican girls, family from Guanica, with sleepy eyes and lips glossier than any fashion magazine. "You're blowing my mood!"

"Chill out, baby. I gotta go to work."

She crossed her arms, and so Roachkiller took her in his.

"Two minutes. Two minutes. Then we'll dance till—"

"Till you get another customer. Go on. I'll go powder my nose. Again."

Roachkiller walked Miriam to the ladies', didn't see the uncool short dude anywhere, went into the men's. Was there shaking the snake, when little dude, young guy, shoulder-tapped me.

"Give Roachkiller a minute, bro."

"Mr., uh, Roachkiller," the dude said. "Can I talk to you?"

He had a big 'fro, bigger than his skull, and a full beard, wore gold Aviators, a windbreaker, and a cloth tie. You get all types in the disco, but something about this motherfucker didn't fit.

"What you need?" Roachkiller said. "Sens? Blow?"

The dude chuckled, tipped his chin at Roachkiller. "I got

something to sell you, bro."

"Roachkiller don't need nothing, Shorty."

"I know you work for Benny Alicea."

Roachkiller was halfway walking away but his head whipped around. "Who told you that shit?"

"His wife and daughter got taken, right? You need to find them."

Roachkiller grabbed dude by his jacket and pulled him into a stall. Two guys were already in there.

"Get your own!" one of them said.

"Ohmp-pfft," the other one said.

Roachkiller dragged the dude to the next stall.

"What's with the hostility?" the dude said. "I want to help you out."

"The fuck why?"

"Watch with the tie. It's the only one I own."

Roachkiller took his hands off, but those hands stayed in fists.

"My name's Ernie Fuentes. I'm a reporter, okay. Just starting out. Trying to make my bones, you know? Listen, you know this kidnapping is all over the news and the police are keeping shut and nobody knows nothing? But you know something, I bet. I bet you and I can help each other out."

"This is bullshit. Roachkiller got nothing to do with Benny."

"How do you explain pictures of you leaving his h—"

Roachkiller kneed him good in the jewels. "You following me?"

The Ernie dude coughed, let out spit.

"Watch Roachkiller's shoes!"

"The police...," the dude said, breathing deep, "saw you there, man. That means everybody knows about you now. Listen to me, I can help you: I know who kidnapped them! I can help you."

"In exchange for what, *puto*?"

"Exclusive...information. I want to tell the story from the inside, get ahead of the guys at the *Voice* and *Post* and...the old

20

timers at the *Daily News* that won't let a young buck like me write a lead story. And it's not just this. Your boss Benny has been trying to make some big moves in town, expand his business, you know, and my guess is he's going to use this opportunity to throw some weight around. That's the kind of news that keeps on giving. And you're the guy that can help me get it. And I will help you."

"Who's the kidnapper?"

"What about our deal?"

Roachkiller wasn't trusting the dude but was thinking, if this was on the level, it could get Tio Cheo off his ass, so he could go back to taking it smooth. Roachkiller grabbed the reporter around the neck and for a second Roachkiller thought of the roosters. "Just give me the goddamn name."

"Carrion," the dude said, wheezing. "Juan Carrion."

Roachkiller woke up the next day at the crack of noon in Miriam's house. She was off to her job at the salon and Roachkiller was hoping her moms could cook up a big breakfast and then Roachkiller'd be on his way. But when Roachkiller got out of the shower, he lost his appetite hearing a familiar voice.

"Of course he has a job now. I got him one!—Oh, there is Mr. Cucaracha Shoes!"

Tio Cheo was sitting at the kitchen table, eating from a plate heaped up with eggs and *platanos* and toast and bacon. Roachkiller's stomach grumbled.

Miriam's mom, who looked like her daughter except, you know, older and puffier, had been sitting at the table, too, but she got up to leave after saying "Good afternoon."

Roachkiller sat across from Cheo. "What are you doing here?"

"I'm picking you up for work."

"How did you know Roachkiller was here? How you know where Miriam lives?"

"Ah, a good soldier always knows where his target is. That is

21

part of the job. You'll get the hang of it."

"Listen, Tio, you know Roachkiller don't want nothing to do with this. But Roachkiller went out, did some asking around, you know, found out who did the kidnapping, all on his own."

Tio Cheo looked up from his plate for the first time. "Say what?"

"Roachkiller got a source."

"A source? What do you mean?"

"A source, man. Like that guy Deep Throat."

"Deep Throat! For crying out loud! This I gotta hear. Who did this source of yours say is the kidnapper?"

Roachkiller paused, swallowed. "Guy named Juan Carrion. Roachkiller don't know who that is, but you can do your 'Nam stuff on your own from there."

Tio Cheo laughed, food in his teeth. "Impossible. And I'll tell you why. Because Juan Carrion is Benny's second cousin. I know him personally. There's no way Juan would do that to family. Who is this source of yours?"

"Just...just people I overheard at the disco."

Tio finished cleaning up the plate with a last sweep of toast. "People you overheard? Who were these people? What did they look like? How would they know?"

"I don't know. It was...it was dark in there."

"*Sobrino,* how stupid can you be? People talk all kind of shit when they're drunk and high off their ass. I'm surprised you can hear anything in there with that disco music playing so loud. C'mon, we have to go."

Roachkiller looked around for Miriam's mom. "Roachkiller was hoping he could get some eggs."

"I already ate them for you. Don't worry, you can get pizza where we're going."

At least it wasn't a basement.

Sitting at a back table in Pizza Palace II, on Myrtle Avenue,

Roachkiller was stuffing a double stack of pizza slices into his mouth. Next to the table some kid was playing the arcade game, and it was making this loud *wocka-wocka-wocka* sound like a drill in the head, and Tio Cheo got up and unplugged the machine and told the kid to get lost.

Pedro, the guy with one solid eyebrow across his face who ran the place, said, "Like I was saying, I didn't see nothing."

"Not a young piece of ass, hanging around playing one of these stupid machines?"

"Only boys waste their money with that crap. The sound drives me crazy all day long, but it's a big moneymaker."

"Any pretty girls hanging around at all?"

"Nah. It was late. Just a bunch of guys, you know, the usual crowd. I was just waiting for Benny to make his pickup."

Roachkiller stopped chewing, his mouth half full of hot, delicious cheese, oil, and sauce. "It was a regular pickup?"

"Yeah, so?"

"So somebody knew he was going to be here. So the people who did this must know his schedule. That could make it— what do they call it?—an inside job."

Tio Cheo shook his head. "Nah. People in the neighborhood know Benny's face. Doesn't have to be someone inside. Anyway, by the sound of these people, I think it was just a spur-of-the-moment robbery that turned into a SNAFU."

"But it's possible."

"Don't look for trouble where there isn't. These kinds of people are not that smart, or else they wouldn't be messing with the Godfather."

Just then the guy behind the counter said there was a phone call for Cheo. "It's Johnny D."

Tio Cheo went to go to the phone.

"Pedro, can you get Roachkiller one of them calzones? You don't gotta heat it up."

Tio Cheo came back to the table at the same time as the calzone. "Take that to go. We gotta split."

23

In the car, Tio rolled down the automatic windows. He was too cheap to use the AC. He said, "Listen, *sobrino*. You know how to use a gun, right?"

"Yeah. Of course. But why?"

"Look in the glove department."

Roachkiller opened it and found a .38 wrapped in old tighty whities. "What the fuck?! Are these clean?" Roachkiller said, picking them up with the tips of his fingers.

"Of course they're clean. Except for the gun oil skidmark, ha ha!"

"Oh man," Roachkiller said, just wanting to wash his hands.

"Stop being a pussy. Now listen, *sobrino*. The only good thing about the Marines was they taught us how to kill people like we was in school. Tonight you're going to bust your murder cherry. Ha ha ha. Just kidding, man. You should see your face."

"You're not funny, Tio."

"You won't need to use the gun tonight, boy. You're just a little latrine-green recruit, remember, wet behind the ass, and normally I wouldn't even let you have bullets. But, you know, just in case. C'mon, stop looking like you just shit on yourself. You knew this is what we're leading up to. Relax. Let's go to your house. I could use a home-cooked meal and no one makes *arroz con habichuelas* better than your grandma."

Back then Roachkiller lived with Abuela and Moms in the same tiny apartment Roachkiller grew up in, two blocks from the BQE. You could hear the cars and trucks all night. Our windows was always black from the exhaust. We had a little kitchen and little kitchen table, but we kept the seat at the front empty for Papi, god have him in heaven. But when Tio Cheo came around, he always liked to take that seat, like he was king of the castle. Our one-bedroom castle.

"I need more rice and beans," Cheo said to Abuela. "I shouldn't have to ask, since I pay for them." He laughed by himself.

Abuela was quiet, like she always was when Tio was around. She filled his plate with more *arroz con habichuelas* and added two more pieces of chicken without waiting to be asked.

Mami was out at her second job at the factory. She only came home to shower and sleep nowadays.

"I got your grandson working now," he said. "Real man's work. You should be proud of him."

Abuela looked at me straight in the eyes and then looked away.

Tio finished the last of our beer and said, "You better change. For what we gotta do tonight, you need to look less like John Travolta." He smacked Roachkiller in the back of the head.

Roachkiller shrugged and fix his hair.

"I'll pick you up tonight," Tio said. "Right now, I gotta pay a visit to my Dominican friends."

Roachkiller needed to get his head clear. It was a cool day for July, so Roachkiller picked up some roses, walked to the Unisex Beauty Salon in Bushwick.

All the ladies said, "Hiii!" when Roachkiller walked in. "Oh look at that!" one said. "Those are beautiful!" another one said about the flowers. "Gorgeous!"

Miriam said, "What the hell are you doing here?" She and the lady she was working on, her head wrapped in curlers, both stared at me.

"Roachkiller just thought it'd be nice to walk you home from work."

She was trying to be fake-angry at Roachkiller, but her eyes were all on the flowers. "Walk me home? You never did that before."

"You're lucky, sweetheart," the curler lady said, "My husband hasn't brought me flowers in years. On account of inflation, he says."

Miriam took the flowers and Roachkiller waited in the shop a half hour before she was ready to go.

"Have a good time," the ladies of the salon said after us. "Gorgeous flowers!"

Roachkiller and his girl walked slowly back to her place, she carrying the roses, me holding her hand. We was small-talking, enjoying the spicy smell of summer, enjoying the music of the neighborhood. If Tio came looking for Roachkiller, Tio could wait.

At Miriam's house, her moms saw the flowers and said she suddenly remembered she had a bingo game that night and took off.

In Miriam's room, through the open window we heard someone playing Rose Royce. "Wishing on a Star."

"Someone's having a good time out there," Roachkiller said.

"Someone's having a good time in here," Miriam said.

Those glossy lips were sweeter than a Jolly Rancher and got Roachkiller higher than he'd thought he could ever get.

Two hours later, the mood kind of changed.

"Are you freaking kidding me?" Miriam said. She was pissed and didn't bother to cover herself with a sheet.

"It's just tonight. It's just this one thing. It's my uncle. He's an asshole but he's done a lot for the family. I owe him."

"No, no, no, no, no," she said, lighting a cigarette and then pointing it at Roachkiller. "You don't owe him shit. You understand what he wants you to do—he gave you a fucking gun, RK. Wrapped in his dirty underwear! Baby, you have to get out of this. You can't keep going down this road. It's bad enough you selling drugs."

"Bad enough. Wait up—"

"What do you think, I like dating a drug dealer?"

"Whoa, whoa, whoa, Miriam. I—Roachkiller thought you understood."

"Listen to me, boy! Have I liked not having to lie to get food stamps to survive? Have I liked the extra money you give me?

Have I liked the good times? Yeah, sure. A little danger is fun. There's advantages. It's nice. But you can't do this forever. If the cops don't get you—"

"Nah, the cops won't get me—"

"If the cops don't get you, another drug dealer will. And now this?"

"Give me a break!"

"You don't get it, RK, you don't listen to me. I've been lucky and I've been smart. I finished high school, I live with my parents but I don't have to. I got no kids and I ain't never been pregnant. Knock on wood! I'm halfway out of this stinking neighborhood, but you're the only thing holding me here like a chain around my heart. Now I want to take you with me—you don't know how much, RK, you really don't know—but you have to meet me halfway."

"Miriam—"

"You stay. You stay tonight or you go and don't come back."

Roachkiller slid out the bed, put on his Sergio Valentes. "Miriam, baby, Roachkiller's got to go."

Back at home, Roachkiller played some Euro-disco remixes on the stereo, put on black slacks, black turtleneck, black leather jacket. The last few days had been chilly for July. Then Roachkiller put on my new black roachkiller boots and sat in the living room, staring at the painting of Christ on the wall looking depressed, and waited for Tio to honk for him to run out.

Abuela was snoring on the couch, the *novela* on the TV was watching her.

The phone rang and Roachkiller jumped and got it. Maybe something bad happened.

"Yo."

"Roachkiller. It's Ernie. Ernie Fuentes. You know—the reporter."

"What you want?"

"I'm not going to ask for any info, okay? I know what's going down tonight. I know the dropoff is going to happen by the waterfront, and I know when it's going to happen."

"So? What you bother me for?"

"I just think I should tell you: Watch your back."

"You threatening me, man?"

"No, no. Pay attention. Benny has been making moves all over Brooklyn, and he's aggravating people, pissing them off. And the thing is something stinks inside Benny's crew. I don't know who it is, but word is someone is not kosher and may try to take over, you know, and tonight when all this shit goes down, well, that could be a great chance for somebody to jump to the front of the line, you know?"

"Why you telling me this? I don't know you."

"So you can see that working with me can be more useful to you than not. I'll be in touch."

"I won't be doing this anymore after tonight."

"Heard that before. You gotta pick your allies now. I'll be in touch."

Roachkiller hung up slowly. Tio was honking.

Just as Roachkiller opened the door, Abuela took his hands in her knotted-up, angel-soft hands and said, *"Respeta a tu tío, pero cuídate, mi amor."*

Roachkiller kissed her and went out.

Six men stood on the roof of an abandoned warehouse across from the Domino Factory. You could see the dropoff point easy from where we were: a garbage can in the middle of the block on Kent Avenue.

"It's a good spot to pick," Johnny D. said. "No one comes down here but hookers, and truckers and Hasids looking for the hookers. But our friends with the Feds have brushed them a little farther down tonight. Streets are wide but break off into a bunch of side streets. Good for a getaway. I couldn't pick a better spot myself."

Roachkiller took a long look at the small crew. Two he knew from around the way: Benjy, a half-Irish dude who started a protection racket in second grade, and Carmelo, who had a beard and wild hair like Serpico, smoked pot nonstop. Then there was Paco, straight from the island with no English and a scar straight across his throat. They made Roachkiller think about what Fuentes had said. Any of these jamokes could be a sellout. Then there was Johnny D. Benny's number one lieutenant. Maybe he was looking to move up in the world.

For a long time the six of them stood on the roof, and a long bunch of nothing happened.

Then about a quarter to eleven, Benny's Buick pulled up to the garbage can. He got out and threw a bowling ball bag on top of the trash.

"The cops ask where he got the money?" Tio Cheo said.

"They know not to," Johnny D. said.

Benny's car pulled away, twenty minutes later a brown sedan pulled up. The back window opened up and a guy tried to reach for the bowling ball bag but it was in too deep. He opened the door, but got stuck because he was halfway out the window. Someone from the other side got out, ran to the garbage and got the bag. Then they all piled in and the car took off slowly.

Two blocks down Kent, coming from Greenpoint, Roachkiller could see in the binoculars an unmarked cop car slowly moving forward to follow not too close.

"Kid. C'mon."

We all rushed to the other side of the roof. The brown car was booking at top speed, but then, there at a corner, four big sedans came out of nowhere, coming together fender to fender to block the box. That unmarked cop car that was supposed to follow the kidnappers braked and was stuck there honking.

"Where'd those cars come from?"

"My Dominican friends," Tio Cheo said. "They run all the

29

car service in the neighborhood. I asked for a favor."

"You don't want the cops to catch who's doing this?" Roachkiller said.

"That's our mission. And we don't want the boys in blue to get in the way."

Tio Cheo pointed farther down to where another car service car was following the getaway car. "That's Julio in there. Wherever they stop, he's going to let us know." He held up an old walkie talkie. "Stay tuned."

In ten minutes, Julio called back with a location, and fifteen minutes later Johnny D., Paco, Tio, and Roachkiller were parked across the street and down the block from a five-story apartment building on North Eighth Street, less than a mile from the dropoff.

"No lookout," Johnny D. said. "Amateurs."

"Maybe they're trying to be incognito," Tio said.

"Right. Light just went on the second floor, right side," Johnny D. said from the front seat. "So much for incognito. Okay, here's the plan. You two get to the roof from next door. Then it's down the fire escape."

Tio said, "That's you and me, Roberto...Roachkiller. Copy?"

"I guess. Won't they be watching the fire escape?"

"Not with Benjy and Carmelo knocking on the front door," Johnny D. said. "Besides, they won't be able to see jack. I'm going to get into the basement and cut the power. That will be your signal to move."

"How are we supposed to see in the dark? Roachkiller ain't a big fan of carrots."

"Have no fear, *sobrino*." Tio Cheo bent over to open a duffle bag he had brought with him. "Souvenirs from the Marines." He handed Roachkiller a moldy set of goggles that had this weird extra stuff in the front. "See this? Night vision."

Roachkiller held the goggles close. "Damn! It stinks!"

30

Paco was laughing. *"Huele a culo de cerdo,"* he said.

"Hey! It's been in my trunk for months. You want me to sprinkle it with cologne?"

"You stay in the dark until it's done, say, ten minutes. Then come open the door for Benjy and Carmelo, and we'll all clean up. Got it?"

The others said they did.

"You got it, kid?"

"Sure thing," Roachkiller said.

Roachkiller and Tio Cheo got out, went to the building next door. Roachkiller tried to keep a ballad in his head, to keep him cool, calm, Yvonne Elliman or something. But instead the *thump-thump thump-thump thump-thump* "Chase" dance mix from *Midnight Express* played on repeat.

Up the stairs to the top floor, Tio kicked the door wide open.

"Wasn't even locked."

"A good sign," he said. "Let's go."

They walked over to the next building and tiptoed Bruce Lee-style to the edge of the roof and looked over.

"When those lights go, we go. I'll do all the work. Just watch my six."

"Your six what?"

"Behind me. Watch behind me."

"Why didn't you just say that?"

"C'mon, boy. And don't worry. I got an extra eye to watch out for you. Okay?"

Roachkiller was not okay. But Roachkiller said he was.

Tio checked his gun again and put on the goggles. Palms sweating in the cool night, Roachkiller did the same. The world went Hulk green, and everything that was in the dark was visible. But, damn, those goggles smelled.

They looked over the side, waited—and then in a snap all the lights down the side of the building went dark.

"Go."

Over the side and onto the fire escape they went.

Roachkiller had known his uncle was a tough guy, but mostly as a big *bruto*. He had never seen him in action until now. Tio kicked the screen out of the window, then flipped the window wide open like Sammartino throwing Professor Tanaka over the ropes.

In the green light, Roachkiller saw three men at the apartment's front door, yelling for whoever was on the other side to go away.

The plan was working. They didn't see Tio coming.

Tio took out the first one with a shot to the back of the head, the red of the blood looking black in the goggles. Tio turned and shot the second man in the chest and face. The third man shot wildly at the wall. Tio calmly, professionally walked right up to him in the darkness and shot him in the face.

A shadow came from behind Roachkiller and jumped Tio. Damn, Roachkiller was supposed to watch his six, his six!

Roachkiller tried to help, got in there to pull the shadow off, but we all went down in a tumble, crashing something. The shadow—the man who had run out of the getaway car—he yanked off Tio's goggles and smacked him in the face with them. Roachkiller tried to aim his gun, but hesitated. Would he hit Tio?

Then with a snap the lights went back on. Was that ten minutes? So fast?

Roachkiller stood there useless when a knife the size of skateboard was in Tio's hand and it flashed up in into the man's torso, just under his armpit.

"Get this son of bitch off of me, *sobrino*."

Roachkiller pulled the heavy body off, was bending down to give Tio back his goggles. What happened next took less than two seconds, but it stretched out to forever.

A young girl ran into the room, about fourteen, with long, black hair, yelling.

Lydia. Must be, Roachkiller figured, Benny's daughter. How did she get free?

"Embustero!" she screamed. *"Come mierda!"*

There was a gun in her hand and Tio, who a minute before had moved like lightning didn't react, stood there, was shot one-two-three in the face. Roachkiller reacted, not thinking, just reacted. She was turning to him, still screaming, not words, just screaming.

Roachkiller shot once, didn't even see where the bullet went. She fell to the floor.

The apartment was quiet now.

The decoy girl outside of the pizzeria. That was who she was. That was who she better be. Her life was gone. And Tio had been right. It had been easy. You just had to be calm and professional about it. And not throw up like Roachkiller wanted to.

Roachkiller looked around. It was regular apartment, a couch, a coffee table, now broken, a TV set, now busted. Regular except for the dead bodies. And there was Tio, still looking up at Roachkiller like Roachkiller was some latrine-green recruit, whatever the fuck that was.

There was a closet in the bedroom.

Tied up, squeezed in behind some coats, faces streaked with dirt and tears, Ada and Lydia looked up at Roachkiller and wondered who the hell he was.

Roachkiller called Miriam from a payphone on Broadway. It was three in the morning, but that wasn't strange for us.

She knew it was Roachkiller before he spoke.

"I got nothing to say to you," she said. Rough-edged, sleepy, her magic, sexy middle-of-the-night voice. But there was no flirt in it, no piece of a dream. "What, you got nothing to say? You're an obscene caller now, too?"

Roachkiller almost busted out laughing, Miriam could always make him laugh, but Roachkiller stayed quiet. Miriam had a chain around her heart that needed to break.

"Why don't you hang up?" she said. "No? I'll do it for you.

Don't call back, RK. Don't come to the shop. Don't ever contact me ever again."

Roachkiller wasn't sad. Wasn't angry. Didn't feel nothing. Three days later Mami and Abuela were wearing black. They cried soft and quiet and still while they moved around the apartment kitchen, getting food ready for after the funeral.

Roachkiller sat at the head of the table now. Coffee got cold in front of him. It was over now, this business of his uncle's. Roachkiller could go back to taking it easy, spending nights at the disco, counting up chump change.

But there was questions. That girl, she called Tio Cheo a liar. What the hell did she mean? She had known Tio, you could see it in her eyes. Tio had three eyes, and he couldn't stop what was right in front of him. Because he didn't want to?

In the *Daily News,* the cops said one of the bodies found at the scene was Juan Carrion's, the Godfather's second cousin. So was he behind the whole thing? Had the reporter been right, and Tio wrong? Or maybe Tio knew the truth all along?

Whatever, whatever, whatever. It wasn't Roachkiller's business. It didn't matter. Tonight he would be at the disco and everything would be smooth again.

The doorbell rang. It was early for mourners, but people sometimes did that, to bring food, or just to be there.

At the door was Johnny D., dressed in baby blue, shades hiding his eyes. "No questions," he said. "Let's go."

In the car the radio was playing Hector Lavoe, and there was time to think. Only one person could have put those lights back on so quickly. Maybe they couldn't see how things might go exactly, but they knew it would be a SNAFU no matter what.

Roachkiller watched Johnny D. drive.

"Yeah, when those lights came back on, it scared the shit out of me," Roachkiller said.

"The landlord suddenly came down," Johnny D. said. "I had

to get out of there, understand? No choice."

"I understand."

In the pizzeria, there was an office behind the kitchen that Roachkiller had never seen before. On a leather couch there was Benny, in white slacks, a black guayabera, and red roachkiller boots.

"There he is. Mr. Roachkiller. See? I like your taste in clothes."

Johnny D. took a seat, lit a cigarette.

No one offered a seat, so Roachkiller stood there. "Yeah."

"First of all, I want to offer my condolences. Your uncle occupied a special place in my heart and in my business. You won't have to reach into your pocket for the funeral neither. I'll take care of that. He'll get the best. The best!"

Roachkiller didn't know if he should thank Benny, just nodded.

"That said, with Cheo gone, there is now an opening available for someone young and willing to learn."

Roachkiller was about to say "Hell, no, smell you later," spin on the heels of his boots, and book back to the funeral. Say goodbye to Tio Cheo and his life.

But Tio was still family, and Roachkiller wanted to find out, had to find out what really happened to him. And Roachkiller knew it had something to do with that slick Johnny D.

"You would be working with Johnny," the Godfather said then.

Johnny D. smiled, blew smoke circles up to the ceiling. "That's right, kid. I'll show you the ropes."

That was it. That was how Roachkiller would get his answers. That was the day, the moment, the second Roachkiller really became whoever he is today.

"Okay. I'm in," Roachkiller said.

MERRY XMAS FROM ORCHARD BEACH

Holding her smartphone with one hand and steering her SUV with the other, Heather Rincon simultaneously tapped Tito's number and U-turned to park in front of his crappy house on Crosby Avenue. She was on her way to doing something right, finally.

"Merry Christmas, spazzbucket," she yelled into the phone. Pear-shaped and stocky, she wore her thick hair in braids under a baseball cap. Across her right forearm in fancy script flowed the name "Giselly," inside a heart. Around her other arm, hands pressed together holding prayer beads above one word: "JESUS."

"What time is it?" Tito said over the phone, yawning.

"Time to wake the hell up, bro."

He mumbled that he needed a few more minutes.

"Did you get wasted last night?" she said. "I told you not to get wasted. You need to be sharp today. Sharp? Look who I'm talking to."

"I'm coming. I'm coming. Damn!"

The Bronx streets shone wet from the previous night's pathetic attempt at snowfall. Above Heather, the sky was a dull black, layered with slate gray clouds. At just past six in the morning, people were already out, probably on their way to the bakery to get pies and cookies and all that fattening crap for Christmas dinner. Heather drummed her hands on the steering wheel, then surfed through radio stations. She kept hearing snatches of Mariah Carey's "All I Want for Christmas," which made her push the button faster. Where were all the good Christmas songs, the stuff she grew up with? Even WCBS was playing some new, douchebag version of "White Christmas." But as it ended, Heather was rewarded with a segue into "Dominick the Donkey," which she hated, but which was better than anything Mariah Carey ever recorded.

She looked at the time on her phone and then looked at the door of Tito's house. "C'mon, c'mon, c'mon, c'mon."

A few minutes later, Tito emerged, thin as a spliff, puffy eyed, in a denim jacket over a hoodie, and carrying a small duffel bag and two large shopping bags with nutcracker soldiers on them.

"You're freaking serious with those?" Heather said.

"Carmen said as long as I was going out I should drop these at her mom's because we're bringing food later, and she doesn't want to carry so much."

"Does she keep your balls on a keychain or in a jar on a shelf?"

"She keeps them on her chin, where they belong."

"You're a riot, Tito. Don't ever change."

Heather floored the car all the way up Westchester Avenue.

"Can't we drop these off now before the thing?"

"Nope," she said. "We cannot fucking drop them off before the thing. We're already running late because of you." Heather checked the time. "Tell me you got the stuff."

"Of course. Damn," Tito said and took out the shims he had made from crushed beer cans.

"Good man."

Heather lit up a cigarette, and Tito gestured for her to give

38

him one, so she did.

"What's with the oldies?" Tito said.

"It's Christmastime. Perfect time for the oldies."

"You know what my favorite Christmas song is?"

"I don't have the slightest."

"'Old Lang Syne,' by Don Fogelberg."

"It's *Dan* Fogelberg."

"Is it?"

"Yeah, and it's not a Christmas song."

Heather sped onto the Hutchinson River Parkway north. No cars anywhere. Thank freaking *Jesucristo.*

"Yes, it is. It's on Christmas Eve," Tito said, then he sang, "'*The snow was falling Christmas Eve.*' See?"

"Do me a favor, Tito: Never sing again. Especially that song. It's a freaking earworm."

"Whaddya mean?"

"It digs into your skull and never lets go."

"That's why I like it. What's your favorite?"

"I don't know. What a question," Heather said, then she thought about it. "Honestly, 'Rudolph the Red-Nosed Reindeer.' Fucking love that song. That song is Christmas to me."

"You serious?"

"Yes!"

"It's so cliché."

"Shut the fuck up. We're here."

She pulled slowly into the parking lot of Orchard Beach. Empty. She parked at the west end of the lot, as far as possible from the bus stop and the security guard office. She checked her watch. Four minutes to spare.

They got out of the car and made their way toward the beach.

Orchard Beach, aka Chocha Beach, aka La Playa De Los Mojones, aka the Riviera of the Bronx, was a manmade beach stretched out for more than a mile in an arc that hugged a bay that was less a bay and more the rectal end of Long Island Sound. The water was brown, so calm it was almost stagnant. Underneath it, rocks and broken glass and broken shells waited to stab you. On the surface plastic bags floated like fields of urban jellyfish. Heather had spent many summer days there, too many. Always packed, not a spot of sand free by the time her family finally arrived, usually in the afternoons. Music blasted from one boom box after another, and you had a real mix of the Bronx there, the Irish, the Italians, the Jews, the Puerto Ricans, and, for they most part, they got along. Her father would plop down on his beach chair and drink one Budweiser after another until he stewed in the sun. He would get sunburn every June but turn nut-brown by August. And yet cancer hadn't killed him. Yet.

It was her mother who showed her how to swim and how to get the attention of the boys, both lessons taught before Heather was ten. She liked the swimming all right, but the boys bored her. By the time she was twelve she was filling out and damned proud of it, lording it over the flat-chested girls at Saint Theresa's. Although there was one girl she never lorded it over, one that made her feel weird but good. And when she tried to kiss AnnaMaria Pannuzio in the deep woods facing Twin Island, way at the end of the beach, well, her screams sealed Heather's reputation and her fate. AnnaMaria ran away, and Heather stayed behind, sitting on a log, chewing on a cigarette she had intended to share.

But that summer was a long time ago.

Heather and Tito made their way to the back of the bath-house in section eight of the beach. The city was always threatening to revitalize the beach's bathhouses. A little bit here and little bit there got fixed. But it was still the Bronx and nobody gave a shit about the Bronx.

They got to the cinder block bathroom station, with a men's entrance on one side and a women's on the other. Heather peeked around. One person in jogging clothes way over by section two, and another couple heading into the cold hideaway of the woods. She hoped they had condoms.

"Why the hell do people come to Chocha Beach on Christmas Day?" Heather said.

"You mean they should be home unwrapping presents, like we should be," Tito said.

"Shithead," she said. "This is my present."

In the winter, the bathroom doors were padlocked. They went around to the women's entrance.

"This is the one," Heather said. "Get to work, my friend."

From the duffle bag, Tito took out the shims and began working them into the shank holes of the padlock, easing them open.

"Ow! Shit!" he said.

"What?"

"I cut myself."

"Stop crying and hurry up."

"It's cold out here. My fingers are numb."

"So's your head. C'mon, guy'll be here soon. I hope he follows instructions."

A few moments later, Tito announced he was in.

Dirty white tiles covered the floor. The wall had aqua blue waves, chipped and fading, a tiny window was painted shut. The metal mirror hung broken over dirty, rusted sinks. Cans of paints and paint thinner had been stacked under the sinks, for a job that looked like it would never get done.

"Go find a good spot in the trees," Heather said. "Try not to freeze your delicate ass."

She stayed by the building and kept watch.

She knew Giselly would be up because the kids would be up. Heather wanted to call her but the time wasn't right yet.

It was starting to get bright out when Ledesma finally appeared, making his way up the path from the parking. He was alone, per Heather's instructions.

She waved at him, and the lawyer made a move to wave back but stopped himself.

Ledesma was tall, had on one of those wool fedoras that older men wear even though he wasn't that old. And he wore what Heather recognized was a seven hundred dollar Canada Goose jacket with coyote fur lining. That would have some nice resale value.

"Okay, I'm here," he said when he came up to Heather. "I'm guessing you're supposed to be 'Mr. X.'"

"I am indeed, buddy. Follow me."

Heather lead Ledesma back to the bathroom station. The lawyer stopped outside and looked the place over.

"What the hell is this?"

Heather wondered if he would recognize it too soon. She didn't want him hesitating to go in.

"My office," she said. "You want to complain or you want to get this over with?"

"Ladies first."

Heather smirked at him. "Gee, thanks."

When they were inside, Tito ran from his spot in the woods. He stepped in and blocked the doorway. Blood covered his right hand and was smeared in a long swipe on his hoodie.

When Ledesma saw him, he said, "This must be your partner, 'Ms. Y.'"

"What's that supposed to mean?" Tito said.

"Never mind," Heather said. "He's got jokes."

"I have your money," Ledesma said. "Where is this so-called evidence?"

"I have the evidence against your client right here." From her coat pocket, Heather pulled out a sealed manila envelope. The only thing in it were a couple of folded-up pages from yesterday's *New York Post*. "Money first, my friend."

"You know what? No. I think you two are a couple of jokers, and I smell bullshit. What the fuck do you really want? I got three screaming spoiled brats waiting to open their goddamned presents. If you don't tell me what the fuck this is really about, I'm getting out of here. And don't think you can stop me."

"No, you're not." Heather pulled out a .38 and waved it at him.

"You have got to be shitting me. Do you even know how to use that?"

She waved him over to one of the doorless bathroom stalls and pointed to the seatless toilet.

"Cop a squat," she told him. The gun felt good in her hand. And light, since there were only three bullets in it. That was all the guy who sold it to her had.

"Tie him up," Heather told Tito, who took duct tape out of his bag.

When she saw the tape, Heather said, "What the hell? Where the hell are the cobra cuffs I told you to get?"

"I couldn't find them. This'll be fine."

"Aw, beautiful."

"Amateurs," Ledesma said, spitting mad. "You're getting blood on me. You idiot. You didn't think I came here—"

And then Tito covered his mouth with the tape.

"Hold up. You think he was going to say something important? Should I take it off?" Tito asked Heather. "Might be fun to rip it off and put it back and rip it off again."

"No," she said. "I've had enough of his asshole voice."

The plan had taken time. Heather had always known who the guy was, had known friends of his friends from around the way. Edwin Ledesma. Now a big shot criminal lawyer. She googled the rest. Found the names of people who worked for him. Found the guy's secretary, Jenna Raskin, on Facebook. Found out this Jenna liked to hang out at the Charlie's Bar and Kitchen in Mott Haven. A lucky break. Went there, bought her a few drinks, used her best game.

43

And of course she had to do all this on the sly. Giselly couldn't find out. Heather was doing it all for her, knew that it would save her, save their relationship.

Time came when Heather had to go a little farther than she planned. After a couple of dates, Jenna wanted to take things to her place, and Heather still hadn't gotten what she needed. But finally, after three, four, maybe six times, Jenna told her about one of Ledesma's biggest cases, gave her a name. That was all it took.

Although she still had to keep screwing around with Jenna once every couple weeks, so she wouldn't get suspicious.

"And now we call my Queen," Heather said. She gave the gun to Tito and went to the sink to make the call.

"Good morning," Heather said. "*Feliz Navidades.*"

"Where the fuck are you?"

Heather heard Giselly everywhere and realized their conversation was echoing off the walls. She quickly stepped out into the cold.

"Babe, I have a surprise," Heather said.

"It better be those yams I told you to get me yesterday."

"Nah, nah, I got a special present for you. But you have to come see it."

"Oh my god. Where the fucking hell are you?"

"Orchard Beach."

"Orchard Beach! What the fuck are you doing in Orchard Beach?"

"It's ten minutes away. There's no traffic."

"What the fucking fuck, Heather?"

"Trust me. This is important."

"I got a roast pork in the oven. And what about the kids?"

"I know your moms is there, listening to us right now."

"This better be a brand-new car or something like that. Motherfucking Orchard Beach!"

"Better than that."

"I can't believe this. I can't believe you," Giselly said. "Fine!

Fine! Half an hour."

Heather leaned against the metal of an old fence. She lit a cigarette and watched the cold brown water crawl onto the sand. Another jogger went by. A sailboat chugged along far out on the water, some rich bastard's Christmas cruise.

Under her breath, she sang, "*'Met my old lover in the grocery store / The snow was falling Christmas Eve.'*...Fuck! Tito!"

Heather took a few more drags of the cigarette, and suddenly Tito was there next to her, gesturing for her to give him one.

"This is like being out in nature," Tito said.

"We *are* out in nature."

"You know what I mean. It's nice. For Christmas. Though it would be nice if it snowed, like, *really* snowed."

Heather hummed "Rudolph the Fucking Red-Nosed Reindeer" to get Tito's idiocy off her mind.

"You know the only thing I ever wanted for Christmas was a bike," Tito said. "And five minutes after I rode it for the first time I got hit by a car."

"I know. You told me that story fifty times."

"Can I ask you something? I mean, do you think we're doing the right thing? I mean, maybe Giselly is just the way Giselly is and you won't be able to make her, you know, really love you and marry you like you want."

Heather was about curse Tito out, tell him that she loved Giselly, that Giselly was so special and so beautiful and so loving that she deserved anything, absolutely anything that Heather could do to make her happy. But then she saw that he was smoking with one hand and gently tapping the gun on his thigh with his other hand.

"Fuck!" she said.

Inside, the lawyer was trying to crack open the painted-over window.

"Tape him to the back of the toilet this time, Tito. For Christ's sake, you gotta watch him. Can't you do anything right?"

45

* * *

An hour later, Giselly came up right behind Heather as she stood on the edge of the parking lot.

"Wow, you snuck up on me," Heather said.

"I fucking parked way on the other end, like you told me."

They kissed, hugged tight. They had met while working at the Applebee's in Bay Plaza, and one night, after the father of Giselly's kids had taken off again and after a few mudslides, Heather asked her if she liked girls—she had learned her lesson after AnnaMaria Pannuzio—and Giselly said she was curious, and that was that, for six years. Heather wanted to take the next step, make things legal, but Giselly said she wasn't ready, would never be ready, and that Heather should just stop asking.

"Where's my fucking surprise, H? It's freezing."

Heather led Giselly into the park and down a path to the bathroom station. "Babe, your surprise is in here."

Heather went to hug her again, but Giselly put her hand up.

"This place? Why did you bring me here? You know how I feel about this stupid place."

"That's exactly why I brought you here," Heather said.

"What the fuck is this about, H? C'mon, I still gotta make the stuffing and the lasagna."

"You'll see, Babe. C'mon."

Tito stood inside, hugging himself to keep warm.

"Oh no, Tito's here," Giselly said. "This has to be some stupid-ass shit if Tito's here."

"Here, Babe." Heather pointed inside the stall.

Giselly turned on her boot heels. "What. The. Fuck," she said. "What the fuck is this, H?"

"Fourteen years ago, in this shitty bathroom," Heather said to Ledesma, "you attacked and raped an innocent girl. Now here's that girl, and she's not innocent no more. You destroyed her, destroyed her trust, made it impossible for her to open up her heart and love someone, to give herself completely, because

46

she's got like this space in her heart, and—"

Giselly shook her head. "Okay, okay, we get it."

"Yeah," Heather said, "so now he's gonna pay for what he did."

"H, you retard. This is not the guy!"

"What? You told me. You *told* me! And I tracked him down. You said—"

"What did I say? What did I say? I said I wanted to fucking forget about it. I didn't want to keep playing it over and over in my head. I did that enough, for years. And now you bring it back, today of all days."

But Heather noticed, as she was talking, that Giselly was looking and looking again at Ledesma. His cheek was smeared with Tito's dried blood.

"Take off the tape," Giselly said. "Take it off. Let me see his face."

Heather stepped into the stall. "Don't yell, you sack of shit. Remember, I have a gun." She ripped off the tape. Tito giggled.

Ledesma said nothing. But he looked like he wanted to cut all their heads off.

Giselly took a long look at him. "Holy shit," she said, crossing herself. "It is him. It's him."

And she fell to the floor of the dirty bathroom onto her knees and started crying. Then she started praying.

"Take this, Babe," Heather said and held the gun toward her. "Get past the past. We can move on with our lives. We can get married, live together."

Giselly looked at her with tears flowing down her face. "That's why you fucking brought me here? I'm supposed to use this?"

She stared at the gun. She shook her head forcefully. And then she grabbed the .38. "Is it loaded?"

"Yes."

Ledesma looked at them both, his face red from blood, ripped-off duct tape, anger, desperation. "You have to listen to

47

me. I didn't come here—"

"Shut up!" Heather, Giselly, and Tito said in chorus.

Giselly stood up, gun in hand. "It was you, wasn't it?" she said. "You grabbed me and dragged me away from my family. My family didn't know where I was. You took me away from them. You took me away."

He put his head down and looked at the floor.

And then there was just the barest nod.

Giselly pulled up the gun, took a step closer. Heather watched her there, but she did nothing for a long time. Giselly just breathed, looking not at the man on the floor, but the space above his head. Heather wanted to go to her, to put her arms around her and reassure her, but it didn't feel like the right thing to do. Giselly needed her space, and Heather knew enough to give it to her.

And then there was a chime.

And then the chime came again.

From Heather's jacket.

And then the chime came again and, although they had rarely heard it before, Tito and Giselly knew whose ringtone it was.

"Are you going to get that?" Ledesma said.

"Shut up," Heather said.

Again the chime.

"Get it already," Tito said.

"It's your mother, for fuck's sake," Giselly said.

"Gimme a minute," Heather said, "I'll be...I'll be right back."

In the cold, Heather nervously tapped to answer her phone.

"Hey, Ma. Merry Christmas."

"Merry Christmas, sweetheart," her mother said, her voice gentle as concrete from years of booze and cigarettes. "You doing okay?"

"I'm fine, Ma. How are you and Dad?"

"Your Dad's fine. He's had a cold for about a week now, but he's getting better. You know him, he's a tough son of a bitch. Although he was coughing his lungs out putting the tree up this year."

"I bet the tree looks great."

"Well, dear, that's why I'm calling. Your father would love to see you at dinner this year."

"Holy shit! Oh sorry, sorry, Ma. I mean, that's great. About what time?"

"We sit down to eat at two o'clock on the dot. You know your father."

She heard her father's phlegmy voice in the background: "Tell her to do something right. For once."

"Ma, I gotta ask: Can I...can I bring Giselly?"

"Oh, Lord. Frankly, sweetheart, I wouldn't push it with your father. I think it's nice enough he's invited you. We'll see you at two o'clock then?"

"I'll be there, Ma. I may not stay for long, but—"

"That would probably be a good idea. See you later, sweetheart. God bless!"

Heather hung up. She turned and, for a moment, she thought she saw something move in the trees, about fifty feet out. She stared in that direction for a while. Nothing moved. Nothing. She felt cold and went back inside.

In the bathroom, everyone was still in the same position.

"Everything all right, H?"

"Yeah.... No. We better get this done."

Giselly stood in the same spot, gun pointed down. "I can't do this."

"What? Why not?"

"This isn't right, not on Christ's birthday. I'm a Christian. I am supposed to turn the other cheek. I'm supposed to forgive, so I forgive this man." She pointed—with the gun—at Ledesma's face to emphasize her meaning.

And then chaos happened.

There was a noise at the door. A park security guy stood

there, an old man in a white beard, in a shooting stance. His hands shaking, he shot Giselly right in the head. Then he yelled, "Halt!"

Heather ducked low, and Tito, eyes wide and with a grunt, tackled the security guard, pushed him into a corner.

Another man rushed in where the guard had been. A guy in a suit—a detective? a bodyguard? Ledesma hadn't come alone, hadn't followed her instructions.

In the narrow space, Tito was stabbing the security guard in the neck with one of his shivs. And then the suit guy fired shots into Tito.

Heather looked down at Giselly.

Her head was open and her lovely hair was bloody on the dirty tile floor. The gun was still in her pretty hand.

Heather took the gun, aimed at the suit at the door. She wasn't a good shot, had only held a gun a few times in her life, and she was very aware that there were only three bullets.

Her first shot missed, but it made him turn.

They shot at the same time, Heather's bullet tearing into the suit's mouth (she had aimed at his heart), while the suit's bullet cut into Heather's belly.

She stumbled back like she had been pushed, tripped against something on the floor. She fell under the sink and in between paint cans.

Blood pulsed out of her. She looked over at Giselly's dead eyes.

Everything Heather loved was gone. Everything she had ever loved. And it was her fault. She had even gotten Tito dead. That shithead. But he had been her best friend. Still a shithead though.

She felt Ledesma crawling past her and toward the door. He grabbed onto the security guard and then Tito's facedown body to haul himself up.

"Oh no," Heather said. "Oh no, you don't."

She was surprised at how weak her voice sounded. She

hauled herself up on one elbow, aimed carefully and—the gun misfired. She tossed it at the back of Ledesma's head.

He said, "Fuck," but kept moving.

It couldn't end this way. He couldn't get away. This all had to be worth something. *Do one thing right,* she told herself. *One thing.*

She tried to move and saw what she had tripped over.

Paint thinner.

She took one of the small cans, screwed off the screwtop, then whipped the can at Ledesma just as he passed the entrance. A long streak of paint thinner splashed onto his back.

Heather fished out her lighter, clicked it on, tossed it. It hit some of the streak that was on the floor and lit, spread right up to that sweet Canada goose jacket.

When he realized what was happening, Ledesma screamed. Then he got up and ran.

Heather found enough energy to get herself up on her knees and crawl out. She didn't look back at Giselly. She refused to look back.

Outside, it had started raining. A lazy, cold spittle rain. So much for a white Christmas. Heather stood and felt both light and heavy at the same time. She swayed and fell again and knew she would not be getting back up.

She fished for a cigarette but then realized.

Where was that scumbag? Where had he gone?

There ahead, she saw Ledesma's body, collapsed on the beach, halfway to the water of Long Island Sound, a fierce bonfire under the slate gray sky.

She would even say he glowed.

WITHHOLD THE DAWN

Gladys Gonzálvez hated the IRS. In her mind, the IRS had destroyed her parents, crossing them out of her existence like disallowed itemized deductions. It didn't matter to her that Mami and Papi had neglected to pay taxes for a dozen years apiece, Gladys still wanted *revenge*. From dawn to dusk and even in her dreams.

To that end, she purchased—*on sale!*—a thirty-two-inch Summerfield Tru-Cut™ axe, drop-forged of carbon steel with an American hickory handle. "Summerfield," the slogan went. "When you want something *chop chop!*"

She never dated, never married, never held an honest job. *Revenge* was her only companion. Each year she moved to a new town, created a new identity, sent in new tax returns. She bungled the numbers on purpose, giving herself exceedingly generous refunds. Most times, she got the money. This disappointed her. While she enjoyed the cash, the reward she craved was that neat letter in a neat envelope from the IRS. This meant that there would be an audit. An agent would be coming by.

In Wyoming, for example, Gladys claimed she worked as a safari guide. Two months later, an IRS agent named Steven W. Cabeza-Plana rang her doorbell.

"Miss Theodora Ratatouille?"

"*C'est moi,*" said Gladys.

Cabeza-Plana's hair was stuccoed in place. His teeth were bathroom tiles. Gladys disliked him immediately and offered him iced tea.

Cabeza-Plana said, "Aces," and asked her for her receipts. He sat down, removing neat papers from his briefcase and flicking his pen. Gladys went to her bedroom, pretending to look for receipts. But in reality, she sat on her bed and quietly sang Don McLean's "American Pie." Using the axe as a microphone.

In the eight minutes and thirty-three seconds it took to finish all the verses, the anesthetic in the tea would kick in. Gladys emerged from her bedroom, twirling her beloved Summerfield axe and half-murmuring, "February made me shiver / with every paper I'd delivered."

Numb and paralyzed but still awake, Cabeza-Plana listened as she hacked off his right arm and then his left.

"Drove my Chevy to the levy, but the levy was dry."

Then, as was her habit, she made agent meatloaf, empanadas, and *guisada*. She ate like a one-percenter for days.

Over time, however, Gladys found she had less luck. Year after year, refund after refund arrived without question. She became rich. But she ached with an awful hankering. And her Summerfield rusted with ennui.

So when she moved to Klamath Falls, she sent out ten different forms using twelve different names. Sure enough, neat little letters started arriving in the mail.

Four agents came by in one week, all carrying neat briefcases and flicking pens. The first one did not drink enough tea, so when Gladys emerged with her Summerfield, a scuffle seemed about to ensue. But the agent had spilled the tea on the floor and, approaching Gladys in his wingtips, had slipped, tripping and sending his forehead right into the edge of her axe. With the second and third agents, everything went hunky-dory. Tea. "Pie." *Chop.* In fact, by the time the fourth agent arrived, Gladys found herself bored. She brought the axe to the door and took him out just as he stepped in. Then she did yoga.

That month, Gladys made so much meatloaf, empanadas, and *guisada* that she began selling the extra. Everyone on the block said they were delish. She was even written up in a neighbor's blog, something that delighted her, because who wouldn't want to be on a blog?

It also made her wonder if perhaps the ardor of her revenge had been quelled. Yes, perhaps it was time to put away her faithful Summerfield and have a real life, to sleep next to something warm and soft, not cold and sharp.

And then one day, in hazy August, the doorbell rang.

"Mrs. Feldshuh, my name is Chris Haragán, and I'm from the IRS."

Slouching and unzippered, Haragán did not seem at all like an IRS agent to Gladys.

"Don't be alarmed, ma'am, I was going to send a letter, but I got busy at work, my grandmother passed, my cat got this weird eye infection. Listen, I'm sorry. Here's the letter. I did type it."

Haragán handed her a dirty envelope. Gladys didn't understand. She had already received her refund under the name Feldshuh. Twice. Gladys took the filthy envelope. The letter inside was wrinkled and a coffee stain made a crude yet artistic design in one corner.

"What's the hullabaloo?" she said.

"I happen to subscribe to your neighbor's blog," said Haragán, "and I read about the success of your home business. Frankly, ma'am, I think you're making money that belongs to the government."

"Hm," Gladys said, "Would you like some iced tea?"

"No, thanks, ma'am. Do you mind if I smoke?"

"I guess," she said.

Gladys suddenly found that she was irresistibly attracted to this fellow. But he was IRS. And she hated the IRS. She could sneak up behind him with her cherished Summerfield—so she wouldn't have to see his pallid, scrambled-egg-speckled face. It

55

would only take one good swing to get through that skinny, razor-burn-lined neck.

Instead she began to cry.

"Mrs. Feldshuh, there, there." Haragán held her.

She would have stopped crying but the smoke from the cigarette hanging in his mouth made her eyes water. And she didn't want him to stop holding her. So she kept crying. And coughing a little.

Eventually, the cigarette went out and Gladys fried some meatloaf slices for both of them.

After the meal, he said, "I'd love to try some of that iced tea now."

That set Gladys to crying again. She said, "My name isn't Barbara Ann Feldshuh, and I'm not an Amish electrical engineer."

"Of course not. You're a forest fire lookout."

"I'm not that either, you silly fool."

And so Gladys confessed to this man with whom she had fallen hopelessly in love by his second helping of meatloaf. Hours later, when she finished, he said: "Really?"

They made love half-on and half-off the kitchen island right then and there.

The next morning Haragán returned, freshly showered and shaved, and smelling lightly of coffee and its aftereffects. He brought three Federal agents and a bouquet of freesia.

The Summerfield axe sang to Gladys from the bedroom, called for her to wield it as the deadly instrument of justice it had been purchased—*on sale!*—to be. She ran toward it. But all three of the agents tased her.

"My boss is so proud of me for this. I hope you know how grateful I am. Oh, and thanks for lunch yesterday," Haragán said. "Wink wink."

Although the families of the IRS agents Gladys had killed and cooked with oregano, *sofrito*, and a teaspoon of cumin almost all forgave her on a highly rated episode of *Good Morning America*, she spent the rest of her life in a penitentiary, sullen and unpardoned.

As for her precious Summerfield—after spending years in a lockup, it was auctioned off, then passed from owner to owner, from year to year, and all the while, from dawn to dusk and deep in its dreams, it hummed a Don McLean tune and longed for *revenge*.

MEET ME AT THE CLOCK

Snow! And lots of it.

Lew Betancourt stared out the window and watched the feathery stuff descend onto the cars and the street and the sidewalk. Blankets. This could be bad. This could screw everything. He closed the curtains and dressed as quickly and quietly as he could in his bedroom. He didn't want to wake his wife. They always got along better when she was asleep.

But, with an abrupt cease of her snoring, the great and powerful Magda stirred. Without lifting her head from the pillow or opening her eyes, she said, "Want coffee?"

Lew tied his tie right up to his neck. "No thanks," he said. "You make me bitter enough."

His wife mumbled, "Suit yourself."

Then she went right back to sawing her way through a redwood.

Lew put on his best Brooks Brothers pants—a little worn at the pants cuffs but only a busybody midget would notice—and jacket and then his shoes and then rubbers over his shoes. He took his slightly lumpy gray fedora off the dresser and walked out of the bedroom. As far as the wife knew he was off to an imaginary office in midtown. Let her keep dreaming. Only a nuke could get her out of bed anyway.

In the living room, he took out a videotape box of *The Godfather Trilogy*. He slid out the sleeve for *Part III,* which he'd thrown away a long while ago, and pulled out a fat envelope containing one hundred hundred-dollar bills. He put the envelope in his inside jacket pocket.

He left the apartment building earlier than usual, and when he got outside he saw there was just one or two or maybe three inches on the ground, and so he decided, what the hell, he'd save the bus fare and walk the thirty blocks to the Fordham Metro-North Station in the Bronx. How bad could it be? It was just a little snow.

But the sky churned, as dark as a tunnel rat, and as he slogged his way across town the snowfall grew heavier. He slipped at a corner. And again a block later and almost lost his old hat. *Phenomenal.* He really should have checked the weather. What a stupid thing to foul up.

When he got to the station, his pants wet to his thighs, he ran up the stairs and caught the 5:50 a.m. to Scarsdale just as its doors were about to close.

Lew felt it was only the first of many lucky breaks he was going to get that day.

Lew easily found a seat on his favorite side of the northbound train, favorite because he liked to absorb the loveliness of the Hudson Valley. But a curtain of white hid all the good scenery.

"Some snow, eh?" the conductor said, suddenly hovering above Lew, but looking out of the window.

"Astonishing," Lew said, showing his monthly pass quickly. It was a counterfeit, and he didn't want the conductor examining it too closely. For some reason the conductor gingerly took it and held it in his hands.

"It's a blizzard," the conductor said. "That's going to screw my whole day, up and down the line." He stood there, watching the snow like a child.

"Absolutely," Lew said, watching the man's hands. "A

blizzard." His counterfeit pass couldn't stand much scrutiny. It wasn't even the right color for the month.

But the conductor only had eyes for the white fluff outside the window. He handed the pass back to Lew and then waddled away, looking past all the passengers as he went. "Yeah, some snow," he said to himself.

The weather slowed the train down, made it sluggish. To pass the time, Lew tried drying his pants by opening and closing his legs like an accordion player on espresso.

The train pulled into Scarsdale at 6:45 a.m., a little late but leaving Lew with enough time to take his spot.

He bought a black coffee for a dollar-fifty—*What a ripoff!* Then he looked around—all the other passengers were bundled up, huddled in groups and with heads tucked down. Magda called people like that "Penguins in the Arctic." He turned and bent into a deep trashcan for a copy of the *Wall Street Journal* that lay jammed into a corner. He pulled it out and stood up, looking around again. "Penguins." The paper was slightly stained but usable.

At 7:01 a.m. Lew took in his usual spot on the crowded southbound platform, two cars from the back. He tapped the paper against his thigh, to all appearances a businessman with business thoughts.

A few minutes behind his normal schedule, Warren Kiner stumbled through the crowd and took his own usual spot, right next to Lew. Kiner wore a heavy parka, galoshes, a winter hat with fur-lined earflaps, and the look of a sheep.

"Betancourt. Good morning," Kiner said, brushing snow off his shoulders.

"Warren. Good morning. Some snow, eh?"

"Sure is, sure is. Listen, about today—"

"Shhh. Prying ears," Lew said. "Let's talk about it on the train."

"Sure, sure," Kiner said, slightly embarrassed. "Sorry. Of course."

61

Across the tracks and piling high, the snow fell in a steady thrum.

"Say, I was wondering," Kiner said. "Do you live in the Tudor on Walworth Avenue? I passed it the other day, and I'm pretty sure you told me you live near Fox Meadow, but I saw workmen redoing it."

"Yes, that's ours. We're having a little work done."

"Wow, I don't know that I would consider renovating a gable roof, and one as steep as that, minor work. And are you getting all your windows redone? How are you guys living in there while all that work is going on?"

"Oh wait a minute—you mean the Tudor right by Fox Meadow? No, we're the Tudor a couple blocks over. You and Wilona should stop by sometime."

"We'd love to. Where exactly—"

"Oh, here we go."

Parting the dense white curtain as if emerging from a fairy tale, the southbound train chugged into the station. The train was near to full, but the two men were lucky to find seats together.

"So, yes, everything is set," Lew said. "Mr. Carswell can't wait to meet you. Are you all set?"

"I have the check. And I can't wait to meet Mr. Carswell."

"Cash, Warren. You know I don't trust banks."

"Of course. Cash. Right. Sorry."

"Magnificent. I love to help friends make friends."

"So, where will it be? Did you finalize that?"

Lew took out his cell phone, which hadn't worked since he stopped paying the bill two months earlier, and pretended to scroll around, making sure to keep Kiner from seeing the screen.

"Yes, of course, three days ago. Sorry, but my secretary only reminded me about it yesterday. She's a hottie but not a smartie, like the kids say. Ah, here it is: We'll meet at my regular suite at the Grand Hyatt, so it's more convenient for everyone all around."

"Oh that's swell."

When the train pulled into Grand Central, the two men walked together up the ramp. As they entered the main concourse, Lew pointed at the information booth in the center, topped with the shining golden clock.

"Soon, that will be all yours, my friend," he said.

"I can't wait."

"Meet me at the clock at noon then. And we'll go up to my suite and have lunch brought up. So bring your appetite."

Kiner laughed and smiled and waved and then merged into the crowd queueing up the stairs.

Lew felt great. Screw the snow. Nothing could stop him now.

He hopped down the stairs to the food level, bouncing past dead-ahead-focused yuppies and turtle-slow tourists, and up to the coffee stand in the center. He spotted a young cashier. Pimples. Headphones. Bored. Perfect. Lew lingered there, waiting for the line to dwindle. Just as a woman was leaving, he turned quickly to the cashier before the kid could close the register.

"Say," Lew said. "Can you do me a big favor and give me a ten-dollar bill for ten singles?"

"Yeah, okay," the cashier said, not even looking up. *Classic.*

Lew held out the bills. With the register open, the cashier 0, know what I mean? I'm an old-fashioned kind of guy."

The cashier counted the bills. His lips moved as he did it. "Yeah, it's only nine." In a mumble.

"Well, here you go, here's another single," Lew said. "Wait, wait a minute. You know what? Might as well give me a twenty. I hate singles. But I love twenty-dollar bills." He handed over eleven singles altogether.

"Uh huh."

The cashier handed him a twenty.

"Thanks," Lew said. "You're great."

Lew walked away from the stand, ten dollars richer. It was a simple trick, a short con, but he couldn't help himself. He walked back upstairs, through the throngs, whistling.

* * *

Lew stood at a row of what he figured were some of the last remaining public phones in the civilized world and dialed Bernie.

"Bernie! The pineapple is sweet."

"What?" Bernie sounded nasal.

"It's happening," Lew said. "The pigeon is ready to be picked."

"Oh, Lew. Gosh, I'm sorry."

"Sorry? What?"

"I feel lousy. I mean, Lew, I think I've come down with the flu. Must have been from that dogface kid nex—"

"Flu? We've been setting this up for months. Not to mention how long it took to build the roll."

"I understand that, Lew, but—"

"Men in our business don't call in sick."

Bernie blew his nose loudly, then sniffled. "That seems a bit extreme, Lew, I think. Don't you—"

"Why didn't you tell you felt sick last night at the bar?"

"I wasn't so bad then, and—"

"Well, you have to get here."

"Lew, I'm sorry. I really feel like crap. And with this weather, I could catch pneumo—"

"I'm not kidding, Bern. The trick doesn't work without you. If I wait another day or two he might cool off. I need this one. I got Madga, Queen of the Shoppers, chained to me, and I have exactly twenty bucks to bequeath to my heirs, should I pass yonder this very moment." Lew did half a genuflection. "The good faith roll is all I have left to my name."

"Listen, I worked it out. I called Pete and he can be there. He'll be—"

"Pete, your college-kid cousin from Red Hook? He's no slouch. He'll be smoother at Carswell than you."

"Oh, and about the Hyatt. All the rooms—"

"What about the Hyatt?"

"Oh, yeah, sorry. That's a no-go. I checked with Jose. All the rooms are booked on account of—"

"So it'll have to be in here some place. Gotta think. Nothing's going to stop this deal, Bernie. Certainly not the flu. The Queen needs a shopping spree, and she's gonna get it. She's a pain in the ass, but it's my ass."

"Hey, Lew, listen, so, Pete says he'll meet you at eleven at the clock thing in—"

"In the center, yeah. Got it."

"I'm really sorry, Lew. I—"

Lew slammed the phone onto the receiver so hard it made his hand sting. He looked up to see a cop watching him. Giving him the stink eye. Lew gave him a weak smile and moved on.

Lew went back to the food concourse and had to walk around a few times to find a seat. The only one was in a sea of empty tables radiating ten feet in all directions from a very large homeless man sitting at a table in the center. There was a reek. Lew had smelled worse. He sat down.

He opened up a *Metro* that lay on the table next to his and began working on the Sudoku puzzle. He idly wrote in the numbers and thought back to how he had roped in Kiner. Someone had told Bernie that Kiner was a businessman looking for a way to the big time. Warren Kiner, King of the Kiosks.

Lew had started his routine of commuting up to Scarsdale to catch Kiner on the way down. He started standing near him, getting on the train with him, and then chatting him up. Eventually, the topic of business came up.

"I had a line on a big deal today," Lew had told him, "but the investor dropped out. Tens of millions of dollars to be had."

"Oh yeah. What was the deal?" Kiner said, his eyes taking on a shine.

"Well, it's very hush hush, kind of a backdoor deal to avoid too many, um, civic complications. Can you keep a secret?"

"Of course."

"You know the big clock in the middle of Grand Central?"

"Sure, I pass it every day."

"Well, the world has passed it by. Everything's going digital, as you well know. So the GCRIC—that's the Grand Central Radical Improvement Corporation—is replacing the info booth with an app—and leasing that booth to one lucky company."

"What are they looking to put in there?"

"The usual. A Dunkin' Donuts, Starbucks, Quiznos, something like that."

"That would be horrible. Vulgar, even."

"Wouldn't it? It would be a stain on the great character of the terminal."

"Agreed."

"Now, what I've proposed is that the space be used as—get this—a digital tourism kiosk. A set of terminals with maps of the city, restaurant recommendations, the works. But with a classy look, you understand. I was working with a great company, and I was going to make the introduction—for a finder's fee, of course—but they dropped."

"Well, you know, my business is kiosks."

"You're kidding. It is?"

"Sure. We make info kiosks, news kiosks, you name it, we do it."

"Well, that's interesting."

"What kind of your finder's fee are we talking about?"

"Ten grand. Cash. Too steep?"

"Oh, I think I can handle that."

And that was how Lew landed the big fish. Now he just had to reel him in.

Magda would be proud of him. If she only knew what he was up to. He'd just say he got a big bonus at work. She wasn't the type to ask questions. She hadn't been that type in a long time.

He had hooked her ten years ago, yanking her out of the hands of a bad, bad man. She was a thick, blousy gal who could make you feel like a king one minute and throw a rock glass at your head the next. But Lew loved a woman with spirit, and Magda had that in triplicate. Sure, things had gone sour in the last couple of years, but that was because his luck had taken the wrong train and had been delayed. But now it was coming in.

When he looked again at the Sudoku puzzle, he realized he had got too many sevens in one row. He folded up the paper and slid it off the table.

At 11 a.m. Lew waited by the golden clock. The storm had turned into a blizzard, and the station was packed more than usual with tourists and yuppies. Milling around, waiting for their trains to budge.

Pete would be taking the subway, which could also be royally fouled up by any turn of weather. It was already two minutes past. Lew checked his watch and looked up at the big clock and then back out at the crowd—and there Pete was, emerging from the thickly coated penguins.

Lew saw right away that Pete wore a sleek businessman's winter coat and underneath a suit. He was a doughy-faced, rangy guy, but the clothes gave him the right look.

"Your cousin Bernie always has a problem dressing the part," Lew said. "But you're smarter. Maybe you should be my partner."

"Thanks, Lew. That means a lot coming from you. You're the best."

"I am, aren't I?"

"Where do we meet him?"

"Right here. In about an hour. We'll go to the Campbell bar, make the deal there. You know the script."

Pete stuck out his hand. "Thomas. Thomas Carswell. Grand Central Radical Improvement Corporation. How do you do?"

"Awe-inspiring. I got you the paper, by the way."

Lew handed Pete a folded-up copy of the *Daily News* he'd found in the trash. Inside was the fat envelope with ten thousand dollars.

When Kiner showed at noon, Lew met him and told him there had been a small change of plans. "Storm's playing havoc with the city. But Mr. Carswell is waiting for us in the Campbell at the spot they always reserve for him," Lew said, hoping that Pete had been able to get a good spot in the last forty-five minutes.

They walked up the stairs to the bar. When they turned into the main vestibule, the city and decades faded away. Inside it was dark, high ceilinged. To Lew, it smelled rich in there.

He spotted Pete in a corner spot by the back. Good man. Unless a waitress got nosy, no one would know what they were doing.

Lew did the introductions and the dance went as scheduled. The two men chatted. Kiner talked about his company, opportunity, potential, synergy, the works. Pete as "Carswell" nodded at the right parts like the proper patrician. It was going great.

But something was off. Lew felt there was something about Kiner, something in his face. He no longer had the bright, catatonic look of a woman passing a shoe store. His eyes were sharper, focused.

Sooner than Lew expected, the deal was done. Pete slid the good faith money to Lew across the table. It was just there to show the deal was legit and equal on both sides. All the cash had to be in there, anyway, and real, just in case. Lew had once tried a wad of one-dollar bills sandwiched between two hundreds. He'd had a rib snapped because of it.

Kiner took out an envelope from his pocket and slid it to Lew. Fish. Hooked.

"It has been my pleasure to introduce you two gentlemen," Lew said, pretending that he wasn't checking the weight and feel of the envelope. Now he wanted Pete to gab for a few minutes while he took a quick look inside. "I hope you two make beautiful business together."

"There's just one more thing," Kiner said, and to Lew there was something weird about the way he said that. "There's someone I need you to meet. He's waiting downstairs."

"Why don't you have him come up here for a drink?" Lew felt flush now. The cash in his pocket made him feel fifty feet tall. But he still smelled something off.

"You don't get it," Kiner said. "We're all going to go see him."

"Down here?" Lew said.

"Yes," Kiner said, casual as velour. "He was just getting off the train."

There were on a Main Concourse level but in an area without stores—a dark and surprisingly quiet area for the terminal. Kiner lead them way down the darkened end of the boarding entrances.

"Are there any trains this way?" Lew asked, fearing the answer.

"Must be," Pete said.

Lew saw where they were headed and suddenly knew the train his luck was taking had just been derailed.

"Track 13," he said, more to himself than the other men. "Masterful." Then he looked into Kiner's face. The shiny sheep eyes were completely gone. There was nothing now but a smug smile. Pete's face was blank. Lew made a note never to play poker with Pete. If he ever got the chance. And then he saw the gun, a small caliber pistol in Pete's hand. Which made a game of poker in his future very unlikely.

"Pete?"

"Sorry, Lew."

"Let's hurry now," said Kiner. "Business can't stand still."

They walked down a small flight of steps. There were two tracks off the platform: Track 13, which sat empty, and across, a Track 11, where a train waited, looking like it had been waiting a very long time. Blocking the view from other tracks was a high wall of refuse, metal containers, tarps.

"Exceptional," Lew said. "Where's your friend?"

There was no one down there. The concourse was just a hundred or so feet up and back, packed with penguins bumping into each other to get around. But that world might as well have been miles away.

With Kiner in front and Pete behind him, Lew walked halfway down the platform.

And then from behind a column an old man walked out. He wore a thick wool coat and a dark blue old-fashioned fedora, cocked amiably to the side. But his face was as friendly as a brick.

Lew recognized him immediately.

"Hiya, Lew. Long time."

"If it isn't Stew Zultanski."

The old man also had a gun, but he kept it in his hand, pointed at the ground. "Long time. You look good."

"You look peaches," Lew said.

Stew smiled. "First thing I'll do is I'll take your stash."

Lew handed over the envelope and all of the good faith money.

Stew took it and gave them to Kiner. "Hold on to this, Juan," Stew said.

"You sure you don't want us to stay," Pete said.

"Nah. Lew's not a man of violence. Get on back to Queens. I'll meet you guys at that diner tonight. We'll have lobster. It's on Lew!"

Warren—or Juan—took the cash and left with a smile wide enough to cut his head in half.

Lew forced himself to change the saucer-eyed look he knew he had on his face, just for pride's sake.

"Poor Juan had to commute every morning for months," Stew said. "Waiting for you to make a move. You sure took your time. We thought you'd lost your con legs."

Pete and Kiner walked off, their steps getting quiet in the distance.

"Outrageo—"

"We were a great team once, Lew."

"Lew and Stew."

"*Stew* and Lew."

"Fine. If this is about Magda, I—"

"Magda, Magda, Magda. She's as slippery as an eel, that one. I don't blame you for stealing her, not very much. But Chicago—Chicago hurt."

"I needed to get out of town, you—"

"I taught you everything you know. And you took my money. You ruined my rep. And I got ten years."

"What are going to do? You can't do anything—"

"No one cares, Lew."

"I could yell. I could—"

"They're all stuck with their heads up their asses up there, taking pictures and sending dirty messages to each other. We're far away from them. And this thing isn't loud—it'll sound like a firecracker. If anybody hears it."

Stew was right. Underground, the station thrummed with the constant sound of machinery, trains moving in and out. Still, Stew hadn't raised up his gun. He was getting old.

"No, you're not going to shoot me here, Stew. There are camera every—"

"Stop interrupting me! You bastard. You've always been so inconsi—"

It was life or death. Lew went for Stew's gun hand and squeezed and yanked. They both grappled for control of the gun. The older man pounded on Lew's back, until they both heard something crack. The gun fell from Stew's broken wrist.

"Ah, you bastard—"

Ten years of living with Magda had taught him more than one way to defend himself.

He punched at Stew's throat, once, then again. Fedoras flew. Stew fell back, his naked head hitting the concrete with a *knock*! The fever was in Lew's veins now, sweat pouring down

71

his face. He kicked Stew again and again till he was sure the man was dead.

"Lew. And. Stew," Lew said.

He looked around. The platform looked as lonely and abandoned as it had before. No one had heard a thing.

He dragged Stew's body to the train on Track 11 and slid him into a space between two cars. Stew got stuck halfway. Lew had to stand back and kick and push to shove Stew down.

"Garbage."

The body fell down onto the tracks. Somebody passing by would have to look twice to see it.

Of all the lousy days he'd ever had. He had to get out of this business. Now he just wanted to get home, get back to Magda. The great and powerful. The Queen. He longed to see cover her knife-sharp face with kisses and cringe at her snarky putdowns.

He arched his back and cracked it. There was a smear of blood on the floor, and lying there was the gun. Lew picked it up. He'd have to dump it outside of the station. The Homeland Security cops probably checked every bit of trash in the station, and they could find human DNA on an ant's ass hair.

There was an exit sign way on the other end of the platform. Lew made for that, walking quickly.

The exit led up three short staircases and then suddenly Lew was in the back end of a long tunnel lined with boarding entrances.

Here, the crowd returned. Where had they been the whole time he was almost killed and then had to kill a man?

The tunnel seemed endless. He weaved through the crowd of pedestrians, clogged with the smell of sweat and feet and urine.

"How the hell do you get out of here?"

He took one set of stairs, then walked up an escalator that wasn't working.

And then, finally, he was back in the Main Concourse. He decided he needed a drink of water, even an overpriced one. He went to the newsstand and stood in line. It took a moment, but then he realized the fat guy in front of him was Bernie.

"Bernie?"

His partner turned and his eyes went to saucers—and then did a dance to look at something behind Lew.

Lew turned. Magda. A glance down at the luggage at her feet told him the story.

She spoke first. "I'm leaving you, Lew."

"But, Baby."

"Lew, I've known about you for years. You can't con everybody Lew. Not a woman who loves you anyway. Or used to."

"Madga—"

"You're sweet, Lew. But I'm tiring of TV dinners and having to wring twenty bucks out of you for new bloomers."

"Fair enough," Lew said. "So you came here where—"

"We were going to drive to my mother's in Danbury, but Bernie couldn't start his car."

Bernie spoke up from behind her. "I shoulda got that antifreeze like you told me last week."

"Extraordinary."

"I'm sorry Lew I thought you'd be...gone."

"Wait, was it you that set me up?" Lew said, but as soon as he did he looked into the dull eyes of his partner and knew that the sap had been used.

"What set—"

"You don't have the flu, do you? What was it, Pete wanted to try a big score?"

"Yeah, that's what h—"

"Never mind," Lew said. He had no strength to argue. He nodded at Bernie, gave Magda a half smile. *"Mazel tov."*

He forgot the water and waved at them as he left. His partner looked at him like a telethon kid. His wife looked at him like a hawk done with its dinner.

So. That was over. All that he had worked toward for ten years.

73

Done. Madga did make great pancakes. That one time.

Well, he was still alive. And something that had been itching in the back of his mind for years had been scratched. He'd have start a new life now. First, he needed a drink. No, first, he had to ditch the gun. He felt the weight of it in his inside pocket. Tons. Then he'd have to use his last few bills to get out of town, go to Port Authority, get to Jersey then parts beyond. He'd had enough of Grand Central. He went up the Lexington Passage and stopped near the exit to button his coat. He watched the snow turn the city into a pretty postcard, knowing it would only be a little while before it turned gray and black with soot and decay.

He was thinking he should go to the exit closer to the East River when he heard someone yell, "That's the guy." Then again, "Yeah, yeah, that guy. Get him."

He didn't want to turn, but he wasn't sure he should run, and before he could make up his mind he felt a tap on his shoulder and, sure enough, there was a police officer—if Lew wasn't mistaken, the same one who had glared at him when he'd slammed down the pay phone—and behind him the pimply faced kid from the coffee stand. Classic.

"That's the guy," the pimples said.

"I need to talk to you, sir. Please step to the side," the cop, the glarer, said.

"Stupendous," Lew said. "Stupendous."

PALE YELLOW SUN

The trophy was gone.

Señora Olga Lopez couldn't sleep, had been anxious about the next day's big meeting with Mr. Koch and his team of investors, a meeting that, if it went well—and of course it would go well, if she had anything to say about it—would save the Tamarindo Beach Golf & Country Club. And in turn the club and its tournament would bring tourism and wealth to help save her homeland: Puerto Rico, beautiful Island of Enchantment, which had been lingering in a devastating recession for years. It was, indeed, a very important meeting.

Her thoughts turned themselves over and over. Her body refused to relax. So she went downstairs to pour herself an indulgent dose of brandy with a splash of milk and to cut herself a thick, creamy slice of *flan*.

With her elbows on the cool marble of the kitchen island, she felt warm air penetrating the usual chill of the house. She leaned back and saw the backyard door was wide open. She could see the lit pool, its sloshing no longer muffled.

She knew immediately what had happened. And who had done it. She went to her office down the hall and that door was open, too.

Of course, it was missing.

75

She cursed. For a long time. And then asked the Lord's forgiveness for her cursing. Still, she would not lose heart. Without the crystal trophy, any deal with Mr. Koch was dead.

"Analiz!" she said to her executive assistant over the phone. "I'm sorry to call you so late but something has happened."

Analiz yelped. "I'll call the police for you. It's no big deal. I'm totally wide awake now."

"No, no. The police will turn this into a circus. What you can do for me is to call Mr. Koch's people and tell them we're changing from a brunch meeting at my house to a lunch meeting at the resort. Mr. Koch would prefer that anyway—he can see the renovations and have drinks without having to keep asking if it's noon yet. Then I want you to let the caterers know and tell the construction crew to clear out of the conference room. And make sure that someone cleans up after them because they are slobs."

"But what about the trophy? Mr. Koch called me personally and said how much he was looking forward to seeing it. He called twice."

"Don't worry. I'll take care of that. This is just a minor inconvenience. You know me: Whatever task the Lord puts in front of me, I can conquer it. Nothing stands in my way."

"Yes, Señora."

"And remember to dress up nice, okay? Dress up real nice."

Analiz was about to say something again, but Señora Lopez hung up. Gassy from the milk and flan, she knew she would never sleep, so she got out of bed to plan and get ready. When the maid arrived at 6 a.m., Señora Lopez told her not to bother making breakfast, she'd already had a little something, and that she didn't have to worry about cleaning up for the brunch meeting. She called up her chauffeur and told him he no longer had the day off.

When he arrived soon afterward, Señora Lopez rushed to the car. The day was already heating up, and she was grateful the air conditioner was blasting at full power.

"Alejandro, we have a mission." She told him to take the 52

76

Expressway, because it would take them less than two hours to drive from San Juan to the southern side of the island, to Ponce. She would be back in plenty of time.

During the drive, she tried to sleep but couldn't. Starving, she ate three *pilones*, one after the other, from a bag she had in her purse.

Ninety minutes later, they stopped in front of a single-story, concrete house painted mint green and white. The doors and windows were covered with metal gates. Señora Lopez had grown up in a house like this, had known many houses like this. Except here the front yard was covered in trash. A shame. She told Alejandro she would be right back.

When she exited the car, the thickened morning heat hit her like a fist. There was broken glass along the walkway. A horrible thought came to her. She looked closely. No, thank the Lord, it wasn't the trophy. She crossed herself three times and whispered, *"En la gloria de Dios!"*

She stepped onto the porch and pressed the doorbell. She heard no bell ring, so she began to knock, and then bang on the door gate. Halfway through her second bang, the inside door swung open.

A young woman stood in the dim light of the entryway, behind the gate and the screen door. Maybe a teenager, maybe even a girl. In the shadow, Señora Lopez found it hard to tell.

"Good morning, miss," Señora Lopez said. Loud music came from inside the house, so she had to speak up. "I realize it's very early but I would like to see Idalia Lopez. She has done something very foolish, and I need to speak with her. I know she's here."

The young woman said nothing, so Señora Lopez began to repeat herself in Spanish. But the girl or woman said, "I heard you the first time."

"Please tell Idalia to come to the door."

"'Tell Idalia to come to the door,' she says."

"I am her mother. I have a right to see her."

"She has 'a right,' she says."

Señora Lopez was beginning to suspect this girl or woman was what they called "learning disabled."

"Miss, may I speak with your father?"

The girl or woman covered her mouth as she laughed, like a child would. Señora Lopez could see more of her now. She had long, black hair, straight. Over her thin frame, she wore a loose t-shirt and very tight, very short cutoffs. She could have been thirteen or eighteen or thirty.

"How about your mother?"

"I have no parents."

"Don't be ridiculous. Everyone has parents."

"I'm not everyone." She laughed to herself again. "Who needs parents, really? They're super annoying."

Señora Lopez felt herself dripping sweat. Although she was in the shade of the porch, the heat wave that had settled over Puerto Rico in the last few days had turned the air to steam. She wore a jacket over a polyester blouse and a skirt over stockinged legs—she had not expected to be outdoors so long.

"May I please speak to the owner of the home then, miss?"

"'Can I please speak to the owner of the home, *miss*?'"

Señora Lopez had enough. "I can see I'm not going to get anywhere with you." She hated having to deal with fools like this. Hadn't she worked hard all her life to get away from fools? "Could you please tell my daughter to contact me, miss? It's very important."

"Why?"

"Simple human courtesy, my dear. Is that so difficult for you to understand?"

"I no speak *inglés*."

"Oh boy." Señora Lopez threw up her hands and went back to the car, careful not to step on any broken glass. Her driver popped out and opened the door, and she slid into the chilled air inside.

Right away she saw a red light blinking on the dashboard.

"What's wrong with the car, Alejandro?" Señora Lopez asked.

"The engine? I'm not sure."

"Not sure? Of course it's the engine. It's overheating. You'll have to have it checked, but that can wait until after I get to the office. Let's get out of here."

They drove down the block of houses colored pink, orange, pastel-blue, grapefruit. She said, "This is terrible. Terrible! Idalia should have known better—she should have! You try to raise a daughter in this world, and see what happens. She was a beauty queen once, you know."

"Yes, ma'am."

"She won contest after contest, even when she was a little girl. Little Miss Ponce. Miss Teen San Juan. I took her all over. I had her teeth fixed. I bought her singing lessons and dancing lessons. And now this. Look at that place. Look what she's come to. All I can say is I hope I'm wrong, Alejandro. I'm never wrong, but I hope I am."

"Yes, ma'am."

"The insurance company will just have to handle the trophy. They'll pay to replace it. That's all. I did my best. Take a left here, Alejandro. This street will get us back to the expressway faster."

"Yes, ma'am."

They were stuck at a corner only because the car in front of them refused to run the red light.

"*Ai*, who am I kidding?" she said. "We need that trophy today. Mr. Koch is obsessed with that thing. He's not a pro golfer, but he lost the celebrity tournament here. Two or three times. But now he's rich enough to save all our skins. And I think he doesn't only want to see that trophy, he wants to buy it, so he can pretend he won. And he can have it, for the right price. Whatever brings him to the table. And I need him at the table.

"We have to go back. Damn that stupid girl—oh, I'm sorry, Lord, please pardon my language. You know one time she got

79

me so mad..."

Señora Lopez was going to say it, to tell the story, but decided against it. The chauffeur didn't need to know all her business.

At fourteen, Idalia had been a spoiled, conceited little beauty queen. She had wanted to go to a concert—Señora Lopez had forgotten the name of the band. The cost was ridiculous. Señora Lopez refused, and Idalia screamed and screamed that she made enough money from the beauty pageants and that she deserved to spend it. The girl didn't understand how to save money. Her mother knew better, Idalia would realize that someday. But then the girl went behind her back, stealing money from her purse. When Señora Lopez found out, she made the girl kneel on the floor to pray and kiss a wooden cross to show her repentance. When Idalia began to pray for "concert tickets and a real mother," Señora Lopez lost control of herself and broke the cross on the girl's head.

Alejandro stopped the car in front of the house again, and Señora Lopez let herself out. As she walked up to the door, an older man in a doo rag and rotted jeans came out. He gave her a big smile filled with broken teeth as he passed and then said something vulgar.

Señora Lopez was too hot to communicate her disgust.

She got to the door just as the door gate swung shut. The same young woman stood there behind the screen, this time smoking a cigarette.

"Hello, again," Señora Lopez said, trying her friendly voice. "My name is Olga Lopez."

"How super for you."

"Hm," she said. May I ask your name?"

"Awilda."

"Awilda. That's a lovely name. I have a cousin named Awilda."

"Everyone in Puerto Rico has a cousin named Awilda. It's a

horrific name."

"Well," Señora Lopez said. "That's very sad for you then. Now, miss, I have to know if Idalia Lopez is here. Can you at least please tell me that?"

"This is not an office, and I am not a secretary."

"I'm just asking a simple question," Señora Lopez said. Beads of sweat formed on her forehead and upper lip. "You know, I could call the police on you people."

"You could. You have a cell phone, you have a fancy old car with a driver. He could even drive you to the police station. Do you need their address or do you know where it is? I could google it for you."

"Awilda, listen to me. You're being very rude. You're giving me an attitude, and I bet you don't do that with everyone. For example, who was that gentleman who just left here?"

"Why do you ask? Was he your cousin too?"

"I don't like my daughter being around people like that. I know she is here, and I know she needs to get out of here. Because of people like that."

"People like what? Jehovah's Witnesses? People with bad teeth? Vegans? You should be more specific. My teachers always taught me to be more specific. Didn't they teach you that? I bet you went to private school."

"Listen, I know this area. I grew up just a few blocks over. I knew plenty of people like that man, growing up. Those are not good people."

"You know, that could have been my father, and you were rude to me and my family."

Señora Lopez gave the young woman a long look. No, she was definitely not a child, but she wasn't healthy, and hadn't been eating. This was a sick environment. Sour smells came from inside the house, like vinegar, then a stink like a skunk. She knew what all that was. Then she wondered: Maybe it wasn't this young woman's fault.

"Tell me, Awilda. Is there someone in there stopping you, is

81

that it? Is there someone you're afraid of, that's not letting you give me answers?"

"You think there's somebody behind me with a gun, telling me what to say like a puppet? You've got a super imagination, lady."

"Fine then," said Señora Lopez. Then she turned around and went back to the car. "I know how to deal with you people."

In Spanish, Awilda called after her, telling her to have a nice day.

"Drive to the nearest Banco Popular," Señora Lopez told her driver. "There should be one near the Parque de Bombas. It's after nine o'clock. We still have plenty of time."

She felt warm and asked Alejandro if the air conditioning was on.

"I turned it off, on account of the car overheating," he said.

"I can open the windows?"

"Yes! Lord help me."

Alejandro rolled down the windows and, as he drove, a tentative breeze entered the car. Without the tinted windows, Señora Lopez saw a furiously blue sky and the sun roasting everything, the pavement, the concrete, the street signs. Gray palm trees bent like old men into the road. The corpse of a dog bloated in the gutter.

At a stoplight, a man came up to her door with bags of *quenepas* for sale. She had finished her bag of candies and would have loved to have something sweet, loved to have popped the little green balls open in her teeth and suck out the sweet-sour pulp. But who knew where this *jibaro* had got them, or stolen them from, or how long he'd had them. No thank you.

Across the road was a water distribution center. A long line of people stood in the sun in front of a giant cistern. People walked in the road, slowing down traffic. They carried plastic bottles and barrels. After the recent hurricanes, there had been strict water rationing and weekly cutoffs, and so the locals had to get water at places like this. Walking away from the cistern, a mother emptied a bottle of water over the head of her little boy, who giggled like an idiot. *What a waste,* Señora Lopez thought. They would need that water later. That mother is going to regret that.

There was no ATM near the Parque de Bombas, at least not one that looked decent. So they circled around the narrow streets packed with tourists. Finally, they found one in front of a supermarket. The unshaded area smelled of urine, and heat radiated off the stained and graffitied metal.

Señora Lopez withdrew five hundred dollars and immediately put the money deep inside her purse. Back in the car, she checked the time on her watch and then on her phone—almost ten o'clock already. As she was holding her phone, it rang.

It was Mr. Koch.

She took a breath. Then she tapped the phone. "Good morning. How are you this morning?"

"I hear there's been a change of plans." As always, he seemed impatient. He had a pushy, aggressive manner that disgusted her, but he was a means to an end. "No problems, I hope."

"Of course not. I just thought the change of venue would be more appropriate."

"And that secretary of yours will be there, right?"

"Yes, Analiz will be there."

"She's a nice piece of cake. Yum. Good, good. Yeah, and I'll want to talk to you privately afterward, about that condo deal in Toha something."

"Toa Baja."

"I like those plans you sent me. I like them. We'll talk."

"I look forward to it!"

Señora Lopez hung up and allowed herself a good laugh that trailed off into a long sigh. "Drive a little faster, okay, Alejandro, please. *Ai,* and put on the air conditioner. The car will be fine."

"Yes, ma'am," Alejandro said.

* * *

83

They'd only gone a few more blocks when steam began billowing out from the front of the car. Alejandro got out and lifted the hood.

Señora Lopez stuck her head out of the car and asked him what was wrong.

"The coolant might be leaking. I should take it to a mechanic now. If I don't, she might not make it back to San Juan."

"Lord help me. And how long do you think that is going to take?"

"Not long? I think I saw a place by the highway."

"*Dios mio!* Fine. Let me out. I'll walk the rest of the way. It's close. You get back as soon as you can to pick me up."

"Are you sure, Señora?"

"Don't worry about me. Are you sure you know where this mechanic is?"

"I think so. Yes. Yes, I do."

Señora Lopez threw up her hands in frustration and got out of the car. Again, the heat wrapped itself around her. She knew the way. Two blocks over, then a left.

She recognized a playground where she used to play for hours as a child. Now the rides were busted, trash everywhere.

Señora Lopez realized she was hungry and thirsty and that she should have stopped to get a little something. But she hadn't seen a bodega open, at least not a decent looking one.

When she came to the house, the woman opened the door before she could knock.

"*Hola*, Olga from a few blocks over. How super nice to see you again."

"Awilda," said Señora Lopez. She found she was short of breath. "I'd like to speak to my daughter, and I know she's inside. Maybe this will help." Señora Lopez put her hand on the door, a twenty-dollar bill between two of her fingers. She scratched it against the screen.

"*Hola*, Señor Jackson," Awilda said. "Why don't you come in?"

The young woman opened the screen door and gate and extended her hand. Señora Lopez put the twenty into her palm and stepped inside.

"*Bienvenidos.* I'm sorry, but our espresso machine is currently out of order," Awilda said. "And we don't have a bidet, but maybe I could find you a midget with a mouth full of water."

Señora Lopez paid no attention. The desolation of the room was mesmerizing. Flies danced in the light glancing through the gated windows. Inside, the sour and skunky smells were much stronger. Dried vomit stained walls. Cans, bottles, fast-food containers littered the worn rug that may once have been orange but was now the color of baby shit. There was no furniture, only an old boombox on a shelf blasting music. It felt like a morgue, a slaughterhouse. She had never thought it would be this bad, she had never thought her daughter had fallen this far. Had she really been such a horrible mother than she could let her daughter come to this?

"Can you please turn that down?" she said to Awilda. "It's so loud I can't think."

"Of course." Awilda bent down and lowered the volume a barely perceptible amount.

Señora Lopez forced a smile. She knew you didn't antagonize the enemy, you negotiated, you used honey. "Thank you, my dear. Now, please, can you tell me if Idalia is here?"

Seeing the young woman now, without the screen in her face, Señora Lopez realized that she was pretty, or once had been. She also saw that beneath the short shorts, Awilda's legs were covered in a series of scars, of little dark holes. Abscesses. Like a trail of bullet holes.

"You're very welcome. As to Idey, do you see her here? I don't," said Awilda, taking an exaggerated look around the small space.

"So you know her nickname then," Señora Lopez said. "She has to be in one of the back rooms. Has to be."

"Could be. I don't have X-ray vision."

"Aha, well," Señora Lopez said, digging into her purse. When she realized Awilda was watching her, she turned around and dug back in for the roll of money. Her hands were slick with sweat. She peeled off another twenty and gave it to the woman, who took it without looking at it. "I know my daughter has been seen coming into this house many times."

"Ah, so you have someone following her?"

"A good mother watches over her children. One day you'll understand. I know what she does here. I know what goes on here."

"Oh, do you?" Awilda said. "What is it that you think goes on here?"

"I don't want to talk about it. You know what you do." Señora Lopez felt herself flushing. It had been a long, hot morning, and she felt her patience evaporating. "You...you low-class people, you sit around getting high." She heard her voice rise and could not stop it. "That's what's in this horrible house. Low-class, sons of...low-class people wasting your lives. Ruining the town, the city, the whole island with your filth."

The heat and stink of the room, the persistent boom of the music turned around and around in her head. The room began to spin.

"I feel funny," she said.

Her legs wobbled. She fell. Down into a cave of darkness.

The little light in the room faded into shadow, and then nothing, and then a sound like a thud, and sour smoke and sweat and piss smell. And it was like she was sleeping, but it had no comfort and no release.

"Idalia! Idalia!" she began to call. "Please, if you're here, come out to Mami. Please! Idalia! Please, Mami just wants to see you. She wants to take you home."

She lay there a long time, holding on to the floor in front of her. And then there was light, and she turned and above her was Awilda's face, which now looked very young, as innocent as an angel's.

"Ay, Señora Olga, come on. Don't you have a heart attack on me."

The stucco ceiling spun. The music still beat loud. But she was rising out of the cave.

"I'm fine, *negrita*. Don't you worry. I just haven't...I haven't eaten since breakfast, and all I had was a cup of coffee. I don't know how you can stay in here. It's so hot."

"I know. It's super-hot. You want something to drink?"

"I'm...I'm not sure."

"Don't worry. Your money buys you a soda."

Awilda walked over to a kitchen area and opened a very old refrigerator. She came back and handed Señora Lopez a can. Then she went over to the boombox and changed the music.

The can was warm and half empty. Señora Lopez put it almost to her mouth, but couldn't bear the idea of drinking it. She put it down on the floor.

The boombox began playing a pop song by Menudo. Its candy, pubescent sound was like a shot of energy.

"Wow. That takes me back," Señora Lopez said.

"The song?"

"Yes. My daughter—Idalia—used to play her these songs back in the day, and we would hold hands and choreograph our own dance routines and perform them in the living room. Every day. For hours. She loved it. Idalia was very young then. I was very young then, too. Although it doesn't seem like it's been that many years."

Awilda lit a cigarette and flung her greasy hair back. "That sounds awesome. My mother—I did have a mother, a super-long time ago. Well, that's not the kind of relationship we had. She didn't hold my hand to dance. She gave me a fist."

"I'm sorry to hear that."

Menudo. That was the concert Idalia had wanted to go to, she remembered now.

87

"I was very tough on Idalia, too, sometimes, but I thought that was the only way for her to learn, you know. The only way."

They stayed still, listening, until the song ended.

Señora Lopez smiled at the young woman. "Listen," she said. "Young lady—Awilda. You're being very kind, and please know that I appreciate that. So please help me. I know my daughter is back there in one of those rooms. I know she is hiding from me. I want to go back there. I want to talk to her. I want to help her."

Awilda stood up and folded her thin arms across her breasts. "*Lo siento, Señora.* But now I'm sorry. Because I have to tell you that you can't. You can't just go back there, to the rooms. This place, well, it's like a club. A super-private club. And you're not currently a member."

"What do you mean? Private club? This place? Look at this mess."

"Money only gets you this far, into our lovely vestibule. To go back there, you have to belong."

Señora Lopez was still on the floor, and she didn't have the energy to get up. "Can I ask you a question, Awilda? And please tell me the truth. Did my daughter come here with something, something she was may be going to sell?"

"You mean something big and super shiny?"

"Exactly! Yes. My god. You've seen it. It's a trophy, shaped like a *coquí.* It's the trophy for the Tamarindo Beach Resort tournament. I'm the corporate officer there, at Tamarindo Beach. That's my job. The trophy is Stubing Glass—do you know what that means? That means it's very expensive, and it's very important that I get it back. Not because it means anything to me. You see, it's from an old tournament, but it wasn't doing well, decreasing attendance and what have you, so we're relaunching and rebranding, and we want to keep some of the tradition, so we need the trophy. And it was—let's say it was *taken* last night, and the only person who could have taken it, sadly, is my daughter."

"Are you saying your daughter is a thief?"

"Listen to me. Don't you understand? She took the trophy to buy drugs. And to get back at me for things she imagined I did. She's been an addict since she was thirteen. She's never had any strength or courage. I tried to help her, the Lord knows I tried. But her father was not around, and I had to raise her myself, you understand?"

"I hear you."

"So, is it here? The trophy?"

"Excuse me, Miss Olga, now I am confused. So, what did you really come here for, into this house that you hate so much? Was it to get your daughter or to the trophy?"

Señora Lopez shook her head. "Ah! My daughter, of course! How can you talk like that? I have to get her out of here. We have to get back to San Juan. The future depends on us going back. Please let me see her. Please."

"There's no need to beg, Señora." The young woman walked over to a corner and picked up a small Styrofoam ice chest. She put it in front of Señora Lopez. "Like I said, this club is members only. If you want to go back there, you have to be a member."

"Fine," she said. "And how...how much would that cost...to become a member?"

From the ice chest, Awilda brought out a syringe and a tiny packet of pale-yellow powder. "This is how, Señora."

"What do you want me to do with that?"

"Belong."

"Are you crazy? I'm not going to do drugs."

"I told you: Members only."

Señora Lopez looked at Awilda. Who was now very serious. Who did now not look like a child or an angel. She wondered if she could push past her, hit her with one of the bottles on the floor. But that would be violence, and violence was for low-class people. Yet it would be easy—so many bottles around, and the artery under the ear is what you go for.

She shook her head. "Please, I don't want to."

"Then you will have to leave," Awilda said. "With your

hands empty. No daughter. No trophy."

"I have more money," she said, reaching in her purse.

"This is not Disney World. You don't buy tickets."

"I'm scared. You're scaring me."

"Scaring you? No, no, no! I'm sorry, so sorry." Awilda put an arm over her shoulder, an arm that had no weight to it, was like a stick. But still it gave comfort to Señora Lopez, who found that she was shivering.

"No, no, don't be upset," Awilda said, her voice now cheerful. "You know what? Why don't you go in the back and go get your daughter. Go ahead. Take her home."

Señora Lopez couldn't believe what she was hearing. She covered her mouth, ready to cry for joy. She immediately got up, took a step forward.

"Ah ah ah," and that skinny stick of an arm had turned into an iron bar as it held her back. "But if you want the trophy, that's something else."

Señora Lopez felt a coldness invade her body, penetrating down from the iron bar. "What do you mean?"

"If you want the trophy, then you must become a member of the club. I insist."

"My god, *niña*, why would you do this to me?"

"I'm not doing anything, señora." Awilda held out the syringe. "You have a choice. Your daughter or the trophy. It's up to you."

Señora Lopez stared at the young woman. She heard her cell phone ring. It would be Analiz calling. Or Koch again. She let it ring and ring.

She was grateful that this young woman was giving her a choice. She was grateful that now the obstacle was easy to see, was concrete. She could see its edges and understand its costs. Nothing and no one could stop her.

BLACKOUT

The gentleman's mouth was wired almost completely shut. Also, he had some bruises about his face and neck. One wrist was in a cast. I made a mental note of these as I endeavored to decipher what he was saying.

"My friend Bob was heartbroken over his girl, Jeannie," he said. "Big, knockdown, drag-out, breakup fight, know what I mean? So we decided to go out and get blotto."

"What was that?" I said.

"Blotto. You know: drunk."

I did in fact know what "blotto" meant but I had not been able to understand the word that had come out of his clenched mouth.

"So, we decided on this club we like called Rvota."

I asked the gentleman to spell that.

"R-V-O-T-A. It's Russian. I think."

"What was the date?"

"Saturday before last."

"Go on," I told him.

"We ordered a bottle of vodka for the table."

"What brand?"

"Solzhenitsyn."

I took note of the brand name. I asked the gentleman how

91

many individuals were with him, could he give me their names. As speaking seemed to pain him, I reminded him to take his time.

He informed me that he had gone to the club with three friends: Bob Drucker, Craig Gill, and Paolo Pecorino. I made a note of their names and contact information.

I asked how one bottle didn't seem enough for four men having a night on the town. Was he sure they'd only had the one bottle?

"I don't know. Maybe there was more. I don't remember."

The gentleman, who gave his name as Ralph Mirfield, was about six feet tall, curly black hair, early thirties. Wore a polo shirt. He continued his account. "The next day, Craig says he got to work but didn't remember how he got there. And Paolo woke up on his own doorstep with vomit on his clothes. And Bob says he slept for two days straight. Me, I woke up in an alley, with this." Mr. Mirfield indicated his fractured jaw. "I have no idea how I got there or how I got this. My friends told me I took a fall down the stairs when we were leaving, but I don't know, you know. I know it's crazy but I have this feeling something bad, like, *really* bad happened and that I'm going to end up blamed for it, you know? That's what I need you to do, find out what really happened that night. Because I ask my friends and they say not to worry about it, it was just a drunk night. Honest to god, I don't know if they're being straight with me."

The gentleman became emotional for several minutes.

I told him, "I understand." I then asked Mr. Mirfield how he had come to find me.

"Bob recommended you, said you had good reviews online, said you were a tough guy, persistent. And it looks like you're used to fighting, what with that nasty cut and bruise."

I touched a wound on my forehead. "Rest assured I know how to take care of myself," I said.

I asked him if there were anyone else, such as strangers at the table, with them at any point during the evening.

"Just us, well, as far as I remember. Like I said, everything after we got that bottle is blacked out."

I told him my standard starting fee was one thousand dollars and twenty-five cents per mile, plus expenses.

He told me he didn't have that kind of money because he had no insurance and hospital bills of more than a hundred and fifty thousand dollars. I understood his situation and sympathized. I asked him if he could see to at least six hundred dollars on good faith, then we would work out any other costs once the case was solved.

He took out a check but had some difficulty trouble signing it. "My good hand's the one that got busted," he said.

I left the office early and went home, where I prepared my own dinner. Steak. Instant mashed potatoes. My wife Marianne would have had it waiting for me, warm in the oven. I had stopped off at the liquor store in Silver Lake, to purchase a bottle of Solzhenitsyn vodka.

I poured a portion into my wife's favorite coffee mug, which had been her father's favorite coffee mug. The next morning, while I did not feel at my best, I did in fact recall everything I had done—watching a mediocre movie about the Vietnam War, playing chess with the computer, listening to my favorite Sam Cooke album, *The Rhythm and the Blues*. I played the album many times that night. After I went to throw out the bottle and then wash the mug, I realized I had forgotten to cook the dinner I had prepared for myself. In any case, I felt fine and ready to work.

I concluded that the gentlemen at the club, who were in all probability experienced drinkers, would not have exhibited the symptoms Mr. Mirfield claimed they had. Therefore, it was likely that they had in fact been drugged by someone at the club, for a reason I had yet to determine.

I took that as my working theory. My next course of action was to investigate the club Rvota.

At the club, I noted that the front steps were made of stone and somewhat difficult to climb, and therefore could in fact cause injury.

A very large man and a much shorter man stood outside the front door, while a long line of festively dressed young men and women waited behind a velvet rope. The short man was telling the very big man, "Make sure to check every damn ID. I don't care what they look like. Every single one."

I went up to them and asked to speak to the manager, and the shorter man indicated that he was indeed the manager. He stated that he did not believe I could be an investigator, so I produced ID and asked if I could talk to him inside. He said he preferred talking right there. His name was Dragan Stevic. He was about five-foot-five, very bald, shiny maroon shirt, baggy shorts, a heavy cologne user. During the conversation, I ascertained that he was not in fact Russian but Serbian. I told him what had transpired with my client and asked if the club had surveillance cameras. In fact, they did. I asked him for a copy of the surveillance tapes. He flatly refused. As I was no longer a police officer, I could not force him into giving me the tapes. I asked him who had been working that night and could I interview them. Again, he flatly refused, using very impolite language.

I left the club with no answers.

I called my client and told him that I could not get the surveillance tapes. I informed him that he should retain a lawyer and the lawyer would be able to seize the tapes. My client said he could not afford a lawyer, that he was desperate, and that he was depending on me to solve the case.

After a stop off at a nearby bar to think, I determined that my next step then was to interview all of my client's comrades.

Mr. Bob Drucker was at home, a large residence in the Brentwood area that also happened to be his place of employment. His architectural design studio took up most of the ground floor. He was about average height, Caucasian, thick around the middle, shaved head, shiny white shirt, gray slacks. Drucker also said he could not remember much of the event. He confirmed that he had gotten home and slept in his clothes for two days, getting up to vomit and drink water. Before I left him, I asked him about his girlfriend Jeannie and what had happened.

He said, "Oh, her. Nothing new. Breakup. Heartbreak. Same old, same old. I'm already over her."

I asked him if he would mind being more specific about what had caused the breakup, in order to be thorough.

He said, "Yeah, okay. Jeannie had been getting weird, for a few weeks, months, I guess, and one day she shows up with rope burns on her wrists and ankles. I asked her straight out and she said she was with some other guy. Some kinky lowlife. Not my thing. If that's what she wanted, good riddance."

I observed that he did not seem very heartbroken at the moment.

"I was. I am. I just—I'm a guy, I don't let it show."

I asked him to put me in contact with her. He asked why. I told him, "Just in case." He said he couldn't because he had deleted her number from his phone and all her emails. I asked him for her address. He said he did not have it. I observed that the GPS device on his phone might remember. After a second, he went to a desk and wrote down an address.

I left him and went to see Mr. Craig Gill at his residence the following week. African American, average height, blue sweater, black jeans, earring on left ear. He said he preferred to speak on the front porch instead of inside. His home was more modest, but he had a new car in the driveway, the dealer plates still on it. He corroborated my client's statement, that he had gotten to work but didn't remember how he had gotten there. However, he added that Mr. Mirfield was "stupid" and that they had in fact ordered several bottles of vodka and then did tequila shots. He said he thought he was still feeling the hangover a week later. I asked him about Jeannie, and he called her an unkind name and said it was good thing Bob had broken up with her. Then he politely excused himself and said he had to get back to dinner with his family.

Mr. Paolo Pecorino was also at home. He lived in a small apartment complex in a studio apartment. It was around two in the afternoon but it appeared I had woken him up. Boxes were piled high behind him.

I asked him if he was moving. He said he had found a bigger place. He had brown hair, was of average height, Caucasian possibly Hispanic, flannel shirt worn outside of ill-fitting jeans. He admitted that he woke up on his own doorstep with vomit on his clothes. He said they definitely had more than one bottle. "Yeah, and then we did shots. First bourbon, then tequila."

When I asked him about Jeannie, he said she was "trouble" and had no further comment. I then asked him if he could shed any light on my client's injuries.

"That's just Ralph," he told me. "He's naturally clumsy and worse when he's drunk."

I asked him if he could tell me who my client might have fought with that night. But he said he couldn't remember a thing.

"It was one of those historic drinking nights," he said. "I think you know what I mean."

At my office some days later, I sat at my desk looking at my wife's picture in a broken picture frame. I made a mental note to get a new frame. I then decided to call my friend Lieutenant Mike Saltzman at the police department.

He asked me if I was okay. I informed him that I was. I told him about the case. He said he would do some checking and call me back.

When he did, he said, "That club you're talking about is on our radar. Violations left and right. Keeps opening and closing. Owner's always in some financial mess, probably deals drugs on the side. And there was an officer in the area who spotted your friend in the alley, not too far from the club, but it was a busy night and he figured he was just a drunk sleeping it off, so he let him alone."

I thanked the lieutenant and told him to thank the officer.

He said, "Hey, if you need anything, you know, besides this, you have to let me know, will ya?"

I told him that I would.

I decided then to see Jeannie Lowenstein. The address Mr. Drucker had given me was in Echo Park. She lived in a small apartment building above a fashion store.

When I rang the bell, a woman answered with a tight voice. "Who the hell is it?"

I told her who I was and that I was looking for Jeannie Lowenstein.

The voice said, "Jeannie? Jeannie's dead."

I pressed the talk button. I said, "What happened to her?"

She said, "She killed herself. Like two weeks ago! Don't you read the news? What kind of detective are you?"

I asked if I could come up and speak to her at length. She said, "Absolutely not."

I let it go at that and left.

I got home and made my own dinner again and started thinking. I looked up the incident on the Internet. Jeannie Lowenstein had been an actress with two nonspeaking credits in films. A history of depression. Images of her were of an attractive young woman, brunette, with hazel eyes. She has been found hanging in her room. She had not left a note. This had happened on the morning of July 14.

I bought another bottle of Solzhenitsyn-brand vodka at the liquor store, along with a six-pack and a pint of Old Grand-Dad. I opened a bottle and sat in my recliner, the one Marianne got me on our tenth anniversary. That had always been my best place to think.

The testimony of my client and his friends had been inconclusive. The best evidence of what had occurred that night would likely be on the club surveillance tapes. After a good amount of thinking, I decided that I needed to see that evidence, that the tape could be recorded over at any minute, therefore I could not wait another day.

So I drove to the Rvota club, which was closed at that time, which was after 4 a.m. Knowing that I would have to perform some breaking and entering, and having some experience with same, I brought along a kit that included special tools for the job.

I had to cut the wires to the electrical system, which was located at the back of the establishment. Unfortunately, the box was too high for me to reach and I did not in fact have a ladder. The garbage dumpster was too full for me to move. I spent some time inside it, throwing out assorted garbage in an attempt to lighten it before I gave up on the seventh or eighth try.

My car was across the road in a lot. I decided to drive it to the back of the club and back it up against the wall. But the back of the car was too low. I had to park the car in sideways. This was the perfect height, although in the process I had somehow misjudged the distance to the wall and lost my side-view mirror and scratched some of the paint off my door. But I was now able to reach the box, although my hands were slippery for some reason. This caused me to drop the kit on the roof of the car and all over the floor of the parking lot. It took some time to collect it all again. Eventually, I was able to get back on the roof of the car to disconnect the current to the club.

There was a small bathroom window in the back of the club as well. I smashed that open, cutting my left hand rather badly, and crawled into the ladies room.

Once there, I easily made my way to the security office, which was locked. I picked the lock with my kit, and inside I found the tapes I was looking for.

Unfortunately, there were over one hundred tapes. Since there was no electricity and I had only the dim light from my cell phone, I found it difficult to read the dates on the tapes. I had to take them all. This took many trips.

On my last trip, I lost my balance exiting the window and

fell onto the pile of tapes I had made. I put them slowly into the trunk of my car. At this point, it was daylight. I saw that I had unfortunately gotten some blood on the tapes.

In any case, I drove them home and began watching one after the other until I fell asleep.

Some days later, I found the tape with the time stamp of the night of the incident. I watched the tape several times to be certain. It was a video of the parking area behind the club, which unfortunately was not well lit. In the video, three men whose figures could only been seen in silhouette were beating up a fourth man. It appeared that they were forcing his arm in a car door and slamming the door.

I decided to call my client but could not find my cell phone.

I went to my office and used the phone there. Mr. Mirfield did not answer his phone.

I then took it upon myself to drive to his residence in Silver Lake. It was bungalow in the Spanish style, with a terra cotta roof and poorly kept bougainvillea bushes. No one answered the front door. I drove around the corner, where I had seen an alley that went behind the houses on the block. I drove down it to my client's residence. I entered through the back gate. His recycling bin was piled high with bottles. Smirnoff, Skyy, Tullamore Dew, Makers, Sam Adams, Corona, Heineken.

The knob on the back door had been smashed away. My hands shook as I entered into the kitchen.

Music, or what young people currently call music, was on a stereo. Only one light was on—in the bedroom.

I found my client there, naked except for a series of (likely) silk ties tied together and around his throat. One of his hands was on the ties, another was around his genital area. His skin matched the blue of the ties. He was looking up at the stucco ceiling, not seeing anything. His jaw was still wired shut, but his lip was split and there was new bruise on his forehead. The wrist of the hand near his genitals was still in a cast.

I went to find his phone, searching around. While doing this, I found his computer and on it I found multiple emails from Jeannie Lowenstein. The emails were of a salacious nature. "I love my lips on your body." "My safe word is 'Don't stop, ever.'" Things of that nature.

At one point, she alluded to the fact that they were "going behind Bob's back."

It took some time to read through all the email. When I woke up, it was dark. Rigor had set in for my client. I found his phone and called the police.

Lieutenant Saltzman arrived with his men.

One of them said, "He must have been drinking the bourbon, lieutenant. Half the bottle is gone."

The lieutenant said to the officer, "Never mind that. Go door to door and see if the neighbors saw anything."

Then he told me he needed to talk to me outside.

In his car, he tossed my cell phone into my lap.

He said, "That was found at a club called Rvota. They had a B and E. Officer Kent pulled it out from the evidence, saw who it belonged to. Good thing it was near the Lost and Found box, which was overturned. Whole place was a mess."

"Kent is a good man," I told him. "Give him my thanks."

"We talked to the manager, a Dragan Stevic. He says you called him that night and yelled at him over the phone. He says he didn't understand a word you said."

I told Mike I did not recall making that call.

Mike said, "We're cutting you a lot of slack, Guzman. You were tops back in the day, and you mean a lot to the guys. But you can't keep going like you're going." Then he said, "What happened with Marianne. You have to let it go. It's been five years."

Mike asked me what I was doing in my client's house, and I told him as much as I felt I could.

He said it looked like an accidental death. "Self-asphyxiation.

Happens more than you'd think in this town."

I told him to look at the injuries my client had. He said he had caught more than one john with two broken legs. I told him to look at the medicine cabinet, that with all those painkillers it was unlikely my client could pleasure himself.

"Maybe that's why he went too far," the lieutenant said. "In any case, it's out of your hands, and your case is done."

I asked him about the busted back door lock.

"Maybe," he said. "But it's nothing for you to care about. Did he pay you?"

"Only six hundred dollars," I said.

"Then you have even less reason to care about it."

It was raining and the drive home took some time.

I reviewed the case in my mind as I drove. Ralph Mirfield and his friends claimed to be at Rvota on that Saturday, the 13th, drinking away a heartache. This was understandable. I touched the stuff, but with moderation. Marianne had been the drinker in the family. Four guys, drinking several bottles and taking shots, they said.

The next day Jeannie Lowenstein had been found dead, having killed herself. There was no note.

Marianne had loved the drink so much she needed to go to AA. I used to find her passed out when I got home, never in my recliner. I used to pick her up from the bathroom floor, clean up after her whenever I got home late, which happened a lot.

The case was about four guys who needed a drink. This case was about a woman, who was cheating on her boyfriend, who was unfaithful.

My wife had committed a kind of adultery. If it had been with just some Tom, Dick, or Larry, I think I could have gotten past it. But she had been with Georgi, Stoli, Absolut, Belvedere, Grey Goose.

What happened that night? Did a man fall down the stairs?

Who was the man getting beaten up in the parking lot? Were the others trying to teach him a lesson? Or were they trying to get him to confess? Was there a drug that made one susceptible to suggestion, open to confession, that also caused memory loss? Or was it just a hunting party?

My wife had been killed. She had been drinking. I had been following her. Checking on her. Trying to keep track. Making sure she was safe.

Did Jeannie Lowenstein in fact kill herself? Was she depressed about her career and/or her relationships?

My wife said she'd been off the sauce. And she was good, hiding it from me. But one night I was driving past the Short Stop, an old cop bar on Sunset, and there was her car in the lot. I waited outside. It tore me up. She had promised.

When she stumbled out, I followed her. She may have—must have—seen my vehicle behind hers. She proceeded to increase speed. I did same. She turned a corner sharply on Mulholland Boulevard. I did same, at high speed.

Who was watching out for Jeannie Lowenstein? My client Mr. Mirfield? Mr. Drucker, the rich friend? All of them? Any of them? What about that new car? What about moving to a bigger place?

I had kept track of where we were. I forgot that the next street was short. I turned, the wheel fighting me. The light ahead had been red, and my wife—Marianne had stopped her car. With the slick roads, I could not stop mine.

The front of my car impacted on the back of hers. As usual, she had not been wearing her seatbelt.

Jeannie Lowenstein had hung herself. Had died hanging, a rope around her neck. My client had died of asphyxiation, a rope of ties around his neck.

Marianne—Marianne's body—exited the vehicle through the windshield. She was sprawled on the hood of the car.

When Mr. Mirfield said he wanted to know what happened, Mr. Drucker had recommended me. Because somehow he knew I was cheap. I was available. I was not...not what I once was.

And he kept pushing to know what happened, and the others didn't like me sniffing around.

To be honest, I had never cared for alcohol, barely touched it. But after the accident, I wanted to know, I needed to know, what the attraction was. What did Marianne find in booze that I couldn't give her. I found a stash of vodka she kept in the laundry room, under the Christmas things. That was how it started.

It was then that I remembered I had forgotten to tell Mike about the surveillance tape.

I showed up at Mr. Drucker's home that night, around 11 p.m. He came to the door with a glass of white wine in his hand, half filled.

"I don't want to talk to you right now," he said. "My friend just killed himself."

I said, "We'll get to that. First of all, Mr. Drucker, did you and your friends assault Mr. Mirfield outside of Rvota on the night of the 13th?"

"What are you, drunk? He fell down the stairs. We told you."

"There are surveillance tapes of the parking lot."

"So?"

"You knew that Ms. Lowenstein was in a relationship with Mr. Mirfield."

"He was my friend. Who just died. My god! Where are you getting this from?"

At this point, Mr. Drucker began to become agitated. I remembered that I had forgotten to call the cops to come in for the arrest. I had also left my gun in my car.

I said to Mr. Drucker, "You drugged him that night, which was why he had no memory of how he got hurt. But you also wanted to get even with Ms. Lowenstein, so you killed her and make it appear like suicide."

"You're out of it, man," he said. "I'm going to call my lawyer."

Mr. Drucker slammed the door in my face.

I then went to wait in my car, which was down the block.

He emerged from his domicile an hour later. He got into his red European-model sedan and sped down the street. I was sure he was going to see his cohorts, to plan their next move.

I followed. The roads were slick again. But I couldn't let him get away.

He took a few side roads, then he headed for the highway, which was relatively free of traffic.

He must have seen me in his rear view. He put his foot on the gas. I did the same.

I couldn't let her get away. Not again.

We were approaching a busy area. Up ahead, he could easily lose me. I sped up as much as I could and rammed his sedan from behind. It was not a square hit, so he fishtailed and slammed into a divider. His sedan kept going. An oncoming black SUV plowed into the front of his sedan and crushed it like a beer can against the divider.

I parked and got out. I slipped on the road and got up again. I saw his body, half out of the sedan. She was dead.

It was then that I blacked out.

When I woke up again, I was in the hospital. I was in the psych ward at Cedars-Sinai. I recognized it because my wife had been three times. I recognized the smells of vomit and urine and the mint green paint on the walls.

I found that I was secured to the bed.

After a few moments, I realized Lieutenant Saltzman was there.

"Hey, Tommy," he said. "How do you feel?"

I told him I was fine but he didn't seem to understand what I'd said. He looked at me in a peculiar way.

"You've been here three days," he said. Then he said, "Listen, we've been working on that Mirfield thing."

My hands suddenly felt itchy, but I could not scratch them.

"We got the video you must have been looking for at that club. A guy stumbling down the stairs. We can't quite make out the face, but it's too much of a coincidence. Anyway, that's how your client, this Ralph Mirfield, got all banged up. We talked to the bouncer and he corroborates the evidence on the tape."

I told him he had it all wrong, "All paid off," I believe I said, but again he just looked at me funny.

"Your client was calling and calling this woman named Jeannie Lowenstein. Who it turns out committed suicide some weeks back. He paused then he said, "Her career was in the shitter, her boyfriend had broken up with her. You know, the usual Hollywood story. So maybe that's why your client, uh, got carried away, maybe took his hobby a little too far."

I asked him about the back door, and I think he heard me.

"Also, that back door. Turns out Mirfield broke it himself the morning after of the drinking party. That's what he told a couple of his friends, so that all checks out."

There was a fly buzzing somewhere, making it hard to hear the lieutenant.

"Listen, this car accident. It's bad news. But first thing is your health, Tommy. The doctor here says you can't keep on like this," he said.

I told him I didn't want her to hurt anymore. She had to be stopped.

"He says you're a danger to yourself," he said.

I just wanted to get home. I wanted to see Marianne. I didn't want to talk to him anymore. I wanted to call a nurse, get her to come over right away, because bugs kept crawling all over his face and onto my skin.

HOW TO KILL A BROWN GIRL
(OR BLACK, WHITE, OR HALFSIE)

Wait until her roommate, her sisters, her bff, her moms, or her lover leaves her co-op.

Wait until the cop in the cruiser outside is sexting his mami mami. Bring a sandwich.

Bring protein bars. Bring two bottles of water. Piss in the one you empty.

Pray that her little kid is sleeping.

Stay in the car and hunker down. Keep the headphones on, 50 Cent low. Don't get noticed, don't let them see the Latino features, the thick nose, the full lips, the Technicolor guayabera, which is under a sweater and a leather jacket anyway, or smell the Jaguar 2999 cologne. Look cool. Just don't get noticed. But if you get noticed, look cool. Scope for trouble. This is actually a good neighborhood, an up and comer, Southeast East East Williamsburg, brownstones filled with buppies. She's moved on up, got a piece of the pie.

Ignore the fact that it's your own ex.

Pray that the kid is sleeping.

Girl is threatening to go Jayhoving on the man who signed

the contract on her, gotta show her Who's The Boss like Tony Danza.

Watch her silhouette glide across the curtain.

Admire the picture they gave you. Her hair is natural now, not siliconed, flatironed, brushed, blown dry, sprayed, gelled, moussed, puttied, and relaxed into submission. It's a wild topiary over her head, a crown, a corona. She's filled out, but still walks like a goddess queen empress negrititita, a vision of confidence and artisanal cocoa pulchritude.

Listen to the cop laugh, expecting a little something something when he goes off work in the morning.

Take out the gun.

Sneak up the fire escape. Dark kitchen window. Pry it open slow, very slow—slower than the journey to Mordor. (Not even the eagles could save you now.)

Smell the inside of a brand-new kitchen. Is that takeout on the faux marble countertops? Looks Italian—*Lights snap on!*

What the fuck? she says. Oscar?! Is that you?

Oh shit.

So, yeah, there's one thing I forgot to mention: *Wear a mask.*

What the fuck are you doing here? Coming through my window? You scared the shit out of me.

Think of something good to say, something that makes sense.

Surprise!

Are you trying to rob me?

I was in the neighborhood, playing like it's all good, fun times, high school reunion. Girl Most Likely To Succeed. Boy Most Likely To Get Left Behind in His First Robbery Attempt, Get Trapped in Cycle of Violence, and Get Hired By Drug Dealers to Kill Peeps They Don't Like.

Expect her to know the truth. It'll be written on her face like Beyonce Bodoni Bold or J Lo Lucida Bright.

Expect a butcher knife.

Expect her not to put two and two that a bullet's much faster than a butcher knife. No one puts that together until it's too late.

I guess you kill a brown girl like anyone. Like blanquitas, Asians, the rest. Blood on the tiles, red in the grout.

Go to pick up the casings. Swipe some of that garlic bread.

Expect right then for the kid to come into the kitchen.

Spongebob Squarepajamas. Don't expect praying to help. For him or for you.

After that's done, get all the casings.

Go out the way you came in.

Get back to the car. Take the bag the sandwich came in, the water bottles, one empty, one filled with pee pee, and the gun, and toss them into the nearest garbage, hell, even at her stoop. Buppie neighborhood whatever. It's still a black neighborhood. Ain't no New York cops going to care that hard.

But—and this a big but—you should really take your time going down the fire escape or else you might wind up dropping the garlic bread, get your foot caught in the bars hanging down like a monga blinded by a flashlight and a cop's irate white face in the night.

Which sucks.

Which sucks.

BLACK FRIDAY

"White meat or dark?"

Orlando said this looking at Marcie and her eyes popped open like kernels of popcorn. *Plop! Plop!* He would've busted out laughing but there was a knife in his hand.

Her dad ("That's 'Mr. Arens'") in the wheelchair—dead from the waist down, depressed as hell, who wouldn't be?—had silently allowed Orlando to do the carving. Mrs. Arens ("Call me 'Mom'"), she was the one who actually handed Orlando the carving knife. Mr. Arens wouldn't touch it.

Orlando was honored, after less than a year of being Marcie's steady, to be responsible for carving the family's turkey. Biggest, immensest turkey he had ever seen, browned to perfection, little paper socks on its turkey feet. And with every slice, shiny, greasy juice bubbled down its beautiful browned skin. This wasn't some turkey baked in an oven bag, steamed to shreds, the way Orlando's Mami made. Look at their mountain of stuffing—with actual chestnuts. Their clouds of marshmallows over the yams. Their red, glistening blob of real cranberries. This was professional, cable-TV-type cooking. Then again, he would expect their cook, Mrs. Sagawa, to be a total pro chef. She better be in this neighborhood.

Mr. Arens looked out the window as Orlando carved. On

111

the left side of the table, Marcie's sister Daphne sipped white wine, as did her husband, Roy, who was a vegan or vegetarian, one of those, so he didn't want to do the carving on moral grounds, and their new baby, Rosemary, drooled in between them in a wooden high chair. On the right, next to Mom, who mimed the carving motions to instruct/coach/encourage Orlando, sat the other sister, Joanie, pale as pork fat, stringy haired, high on whatever they were giving her. She had been let out of some mental hospital just for Thanksgiving weekend. Nobody talked to her, nobody looked at her. The family had powerful genes— all cornflower blue eyes, strong jaws, cleft chins—inherited from both Mom and Mr. Arens.

As Orlando sawed away at the steamy meat, he could feel Marcie's popcorn eyes on him. After what she had read, after what they had begun to talk about in the car ride from Princeton that morning, it was only natural.

During the meal, Mom tried to talk to Orlando—or at least about him. "I bet you're a good dancer," she said. "Is he a great dancer, Marcie? I bet he is."

"I don't know, Mom. We haven't gone dancing yet."

"Haven't gone dancing? Your father and I used to go all the time," Mom said, but then she seemed uncomfortable and asked everyone if they wanted more stuffing.

"How is school, you two?" Daphne said. "What are you studying, Orlando?"

"Computational mathematics."

"That's a foreign language to me."

"To me, too, sometimes," he said, and they all chuckled softly.

By the end of the meal, Orlando had eaten four servings. He noticed that Marcie just picked.

"Fuck yeah!" said Orlando, sated, stuffed, his body molded into the buttersoft leather recliner, shouting at the TV. He was the only one watching the football game. Mr. Arens had his chair turned toward the window, his face very Mt. Rushmore, Jeffersonian, and Roy was changing yet another full load from the baby. Daphne and Joanie were still in the kitchen, prepping a feast of a breakfast for tomorrow, since Mrs. Sagawa would have the day off.

Marcie had followed her mother upstairs, and they had been gone a while. He noticed because he needed a beer and wanted Marcie to get it. Not in a macho way, no, because he wasn't that type, no. He was just too polite, too shy to go to the fridge himself and get it. So he sank deeper into the recliner, melding his molecules with it, wondering if one day the family would say to guests, "Don't sit there. That's Orlando's chair."

Roy stood in front of him, said, "Orlando, hey. Can you do me a favor? Can you hold the baby a sec? I got poop all over my shirt."

"Wow, that's an explosive baby. Maybe you better go light on the roughage you feed her."

Ignoring him, Roy put the baby in his lap. "Be right back."

Orlando tried to figure out what to do with the baby. He bounced it on his lap and it giggled. It had tender pink hands, a chubby pink face, gigantic cornflower blue eyes. The baby kept putting its fist in Orlando's mouth and Orlando would go, "Yum yum yum yum yum yum yum," and the baby would giggle. This went on for a while. "Yum yum yum yum yum."

"The baby!"

Mom at the stairs, looking popcorn-eyed herself, Marcie standing behind her. Mom walked-ran to Orlando and swiftly scooped up the baby.

"It's okay," Orlando said. "We were having fun."

"She needs to be changed," Mom said.

"Roy just changed her a minute ago."

"Men don't know about these things."

Orlando felt he had been snubbed in some way and wondered: Did it have something to do with what he and Marcie had tried to talk about? Had she told Mom?

113

* * *

The parents wouldn't allow Orlando to sleep in Marcie's bedroom. "We're not that modern," Mom said, and Mr. Arens gave him a stabbing look.

They gave him the guest room. Creamy, dark wood paneling, thick, foamy rug, a king-sized bed. *A king-sized bed in the guest room! They must have emperor-sized beds in the main bedrooms.* The bed was inviting, but...

But in the middle of the night, following Marcie's instructions, Orlando snuck out from his guest room down the hall to Marcie's room. It was pink, girlie. Stuffed panda, duvet with a pattern of lilies. With pretensions befitting an English major. Bright bold posters of Van Gogh, Rothko. Shelves of books. Lindsay, Inge.

"Did my family freak you out, Boo?" she said. She was freshly showered, he could tell. Her strawberry blonde hair was ponytailed behind her. She wore full-body pajamas with tiny trussed turkeys on them.

"No. Not at all."

"Sorry about the whole saying grace thing. I know it's not your thing. But don't be surprised if 'Mom' tries to convert you."

"She's okay. I don't think your dad likes me very much."

"That's just him. Dad was a total jock for years. He had a big heart and was always open to people. Since the car accident, he's just not the same anymore. Not that he ever would have liked you anyway."

"You're cold," Orlando said, jumping on her. She giggled.

He loved the way Marcie smelled after a shower, her skin clean and fresh. He was too tired to have a conversation about what she had read, about what he had tried to talk to her about in the car. But he wasn't too tired for some fun. He dropped his underwear and said, "You wanna?"

"I don't feel like it, Boo," she said.

"We won't make any noise. No whooping, I promise. No

screaming in foreign tongues."

"No, no, no."

"What's the matter, baby?"

"I'm just so sad," she said. "So sad for you."

"Oh, baby."

"I'll hold you, Boo. That's what I'll do. I'll hold you. Come here. I have to tell you something."

He slid over to her, still naked.

She looked him dead in the eye and said, "I told Mom about you."

"No!"

"It's okay. She cares about you. She cares about anyone I care about, and it was important she know about your past."

"Oh no."

"Don't worry. It's a good thing. At least I think so."

She held him close, squeezing him. She felt frail as a baby bird, but he knew she was strong. Soon they were kissing, and then she told him that she would make him better, she would heal him.

When he first nibbled on her nipples, she shrieked.

"Are you okay?" he said.

"Yes. Yes! Bite harder."

In the morning, after an omelets-and-pancakes breakfast that would have stuffed a family of bears, everyone went off to different rooms. Orlando followed Marcie, but she told him to get lost because she was going to shop online for Christmas presents and didn't want him peeking.

So he sat at the vast kitchen island, having coffee. Outside, rain came down steadily, pounding the trees and bushes on the lawn, pecking at the big picture window.

Joanie sat herself across the kitchen island from him. Still pale, still high looking. She looked just like her sisters, except for the stringy, ink black hair. She had made herself a bowl of chocolate milk and was slurping from it.

"How's it going?" he said.

"All right," she said, laughing to herself.

"Glad to be out, I bet?"

"What?" A snort.

"Glad to be home?"

"The food's better here. Puts me off my diet though." Again, a laugh to herself.

"Oh," Orlando said. "Hey, do they, like, electrocute you and stuff? Just kidding, I know they don't do that."

"Actually, they do. It hurts like hell."

"What? Sorry. I didn't—"

"Hah!" Snort. "Nah, but they do give me drugs all the time."

"Ha. Okay. Yeah."

"So how long have you been dating my sister?" A snicker.

"About a year."

"We were best friends growing up, you know," she said. "Inseparable. Peas in a pod."

"Are you still?"

"Still what?"

"Best friends?"

"I only see my family once a year," she said, not laughing. "They don't take me out for Christmas because they all go down to Aunt Margery's farm and Aunt Margery doesn't want me there. She'd think I'd devour a goat or something this time."

"Wha—?"

Suddenly, Marcie was there, standing in the kitchen.

"Orlando. C'mon," she said, ignoring her sister. "We have to go to the pharmacy. Dad's pills are almost out."

Marcie drove. The rain was done, and the roads glistened and seemed to tremble like jello. Orlando figured it was the perfect time to finally talk about everything. He couldn't find the right way to start, but then she said, "I don't want you to feel alone in the world. I'm here for you."

"Aw, baby. That means a lot."

"And you don't have to talk to my sister, Boo. She's very strange."

"Aw, but she seems nice, a little funky though."

"Huh. If you only knew. Years ago, when we were twelve, thirteen, we were on my aunt's farm, and we found out that she killed and ate a rooster—raw."

"Ewww."

"I know. Isn't that sick?"

Two car lengths ahead, a gray blue thing shot out in front of the car. Instead of turning to the right to avoid, the car sped up. They heard a thump and felt something roll under the wheels.

"What the hell was that?" Orlando said.

They jumped out of the car.

Her heard Marcie make a sound, what sounded like a giggle. On the road, the head of a rabbit and one of its arms protruded from the front left tire. The rest of it was smeared behind the back tire and twenty feet behind.

"Oh god," Marcie said. "I-I couldn't stop looking at it, so I..."

"That's a big rabbit," he said. "*Was* a big rabbit."

"Oh god. I didn't mean to. But I kept staring and focusing on it. I must have steered right toward it."

"Don't get upset. In ten seconds, you did what Elmer Fudd couldn't do for decades."

Her pale skin turning beet red, she cried, kept crying for twenty minutes, big, supersized sobs. Orlando held her. *Was this the right time to finally talk, to confess?* he thought. Maybe it wasn't. But he did it anyway.

She listened, and then she said, "You don't have to lie to me."

"I'm not lying."

She looked at him then as if she didn't know him, as if he were an alien. She turned and got into the car.

At the house, he thought maybe they could make love and so

117

make things better.

"I need to take a nap," he said, as his way of hinting. "Want to join me?

"No. I need a walk." Her eyes were sunken, her face hollow, as if starved.

"Want me to go with you?"

"No," she said.

Orlando went to his room and threw himself on the duvet decorated with a field of cabbages and tried to sleep.

He had met Marcie at a party and they'd slept together that night. He had been dating four other girls, but stopping dating two of them when he found out that Marcie lived in Sands Point, the most affluent town in the state. After that they were almost inseparable. She loved to ask him questions about his family and his past, but he refused to answer. Which made her even more insanely curious about him. His mathgeek friends told him she was asking questions, but they knew less than she did. He knew the next natural step for her to take was searching for stuff about him online.

When she was sleeping, he checked her browser history and, sure enough, there were hundreds of searches for his name. Years ago he had learned to hide himself online and within social media.

He came up with what he thought was a cute way to get back at her for her nosiness. He knew she was a Craiglist abuser, so he set up a Craigslist account advertising himself as a Marvin Aday, a private investigator who specialized in "digging into people's pasts." Then as Orlando he put a bug in her ear about how a philosophy professor on campus hired a private eye on Craigslist to spy on his wife.

Sure enough, a week later, Marcie bit. She emailed "Marvin" at the fake account saying she wanted to know all she could about Orlando. "Marvin" agreed to take the case, and a week later, the night before Thanksgiving, he sent her a news article he said was only available in print, so he had to retype it. It read:

Family Tragedy Devolves into Cannibalism
Camden, New Jersey—When their mother died, leaving them
without money or food, three small children were forced to turn
to cannibalism to survive.

The shocking details in this bizarre tragedy emerged today
after police placed the children, ages five, three, and eight
months, in the custody of child services.

The family was living in a motel in Camden after being evicted
from their apartment early in December. The mother, unable to
find work, resorted to begging, prostitution, and small arms
dealing.

Last week, the hotel manager told the women she had to
leave. "I was trying to be nice and let them stay a little longer.
But I got bills to pay!!" said the manager, who preferred not to
disclose his name. "I didn't know they were starving. I never
saw them leave the room. When I seen them, they looked
healthy enough."

The mother apparently died of a drug overdose on December
24. The children were left with nothing to eat, and the mother
had barred the door and covered the windows. The oldest child,
a boy, apparently decided that the baby would have to be fed
or it would die as well. So the two oldest children took turns
dissecting the mother's body for food!

Authorities eventually broke down the door after motel
guests complained of a smell and constant crying.

Then "Marvin" added: "The names of the children were not
revealed in the article, of course. But I was able to track down
court papers. The family's name was Lopez, the children being
Orlando, Hermione, and Jason, who was the infant. Your boyfriend dropped the surname and took his mother's maiden
name. There's more. But nothing important."

She sent him the detective a check, which Orlando still had
in his wallet.

On the drive to her family's house, she suddenly said, "I know about you," tears suddenly dripping down her face. "I paid someone to find out about you."

This result was not what he had expected. He had figured that anyone reading that news would never believe it, that Marcie would figure out that it was all a gag. He had expected Marcie to say, "You joker," at best, maybe "You asshole"—although she wasn't the type to say "asshole"—and then he would confess to everything, while trying to gloss over the fact that he had snuck into her laptop. But he never even got to confess.

Instead, she took the whole thing seriously. Instead, she'd said, "I love you more than ever."

The thought of what would happen now that he had told her the truth made sleep impossible. He felt ill. He felt angry. He felt the recliner, the king-sized bed, the house with a library inside it, and a kitchen with a kitchen island all disintegrating, all that he had hoped for, all that would compensate for his years of suffering, melting away.

He wandered to the kitchen and outside to the large deck and the enormous backyard. It was cold and his breath clouded in the late morning air, and then he heard something bubbling nearby.

"Hello, stranger."

It was Joanie, and she was floating in a hot tub at the other end of the deck.

"I'm boiling in here," she said. "But I love it."

Orlando stepped closer and saw that she was naked. Her firm breasts were red from the heat of the water, and a thigh that stuck out of the water looked plump. Just then he saw something floating in the bubbling water—it looked like a human forearm. He stepped back, horrified. It took him a moment to realize it was a very realistic-looking flesh-colored dildo.

"I don't suppose you want to come in," she said.

"Not now." He was afraid to move in any direction.

"No. You wouldn't want Marcie to find you here. She's probably warned you about me." She snorted to herself. "Get going. I'm serious. She'll bite your head off if she sees you standing there drooling at me. Run along."

When he got to his room this time, rather than concentrating on everything that had gone wrong, he decided to think positively, imagining what it would be like to own this house, how he would give everything a fresh coat of paint, how he would remodel the kitchen, build a home theater. He imagined parking a big car in the driveway and floating in the hot tub, and soon he went smoothly to sleep.

He woke up to the sound of someone screaming. He slid off the bed and ran into the hallway.

On the landing, he saw Daphne running.

"What's happening?" he said and ran down the stairs after her. He saw Mom on her knees in front of the library and through the double doors he saw Mr. Arens's wheelchair on the floor and Mr. Arens himself spilling out of it.

"He's dead," Roy said. He held an open bottle of pills. "Looks like an overdose."

"But he's bleeding," Orlando said, seeing bright red on the floor.

"Where?"

"Look at his leg."

Roy lifted the old man's left pants leg. He gasped. Orlando held back the vomit in his throat. The meat of the old man's calf had been cut to the bone.

Orlando turned and thought: *Poor Marcie.*

He ran back upstairs, two stairs at a time. Now he noticed there was blood on the stairs rug, blood on the landing. He ripped open the door to Marcie's bedroom. She was posed on the duvet. Her face, her hands, immaculate.

121

"What's the matter, Boo?"

"Your father. Mr. Arens."

"Daddy? What's happened?"

Another scream, this time from down the hall—Joanie's room. Orlando ran. Inside, Roy and Daphne stood in front of Joanie as she got up from bed. There was blood on her pale face and chest and arms. Something red and tapered as a beef loin fell at her feet.

"No, no, no! Not again," she screamed. "I was napping. It was her! It wasn't me! It wasn't me! Why do you always believe it's me? Please!"

Someone called an ambulance. The poor girl had lost her mind. How sad for the family. Orlando was glad to be there for them. Everything would be okay.

He felt Marcie standing behind him, he felt her warmth. He felt her hand wrap around his left bicep. Like a claw. Like teeth.

BOBO

Hel-lo-o! *Dios te bendiga!* It's good to hear you voice. Yeah, yeah, everybody's okay. When are you coming here? We just got a new generator and we got plenty food now. I don't know about cake. *Ja ja.* I know you like cake! The bakery over here's still closed because *la tormenta de la bruja* Maria put a car right through the kitchen, *tu sabes.* But your Titi Blanca can fix you something, whatever you like. She is the chef of the house. Me, I only eat. When's the last time you been here? Must be two, three years. It's not as bad as it was right after *la tormenta de la bruja* Maria, oh my god. *Pero, Dios aprieta pero no ahoga.* You should have been here, *ja ja.*

But really it's better, a lot better. The hospital over here got a big donation. Everything is new there. There's still lines for gas and for water, but it's not bad like it was. *No te apures.* There's always a bed for you here. Hey, you know your cousin Nick? He was just here. Hold on—

Blanca! BLANCA! When was Nicky here?—It's Raphael. *Mi sobrino!—Tu sobrino, tambien.*—Si, the big one with the glasses.—*Si, que le gusta bizcocho, ja ja.*—It was January, right?—*Que?—QUE?!*—Nicky!—*Enero!—E-NE-RO!*—He was just here, right?—*noviembre?* Right after the hurricane?—*Mujer, no me mientas*—No me mientas, mujer—gwow—No!—Oh,

123

yeah, that's right, that's right.—Before the police. That's right.—You're right.

She's right—the woman's always right. Don't forget that when you get married. When are you getting married? *Ja ja.* No, I'm just kidding! *Ja ja.*

Like I say, Nick, he was just here. My memory's not too good. I tell you: Don't get old. The last year has been terrible, *tu sabes,* terrible. I'm getting old. That's why you should come soon!

So Nick, we hadn't seen him in ten, fifteen years. Hold on, let me ask—

Blanca!...BLANCA!—

Oh, she go to get the diesel. She be there all day. *'chacho.* So Nick, he just show up, he didn't tell us he was coming. *Pero,* the phones *no sirve pa' na',* it works one day, then no, *tu sabes?* Anyway, we was surprise to see him.

What a funny guy. He had one big bag, and he knock on the door, and before he say "Hi" he say, "Who do I have to f to get a drink around here?"

I no recognize him almost. He's a big guy, *tu sabes,* all muscles, with tattoos here, tattoos there, even on the neck, *'chacho.* But he got green eyes just like his mother, God have her in heaven. I told him we got no ice today, did he still want a drink. He say, "*Muerto quiere misa,* Tio Luis." What a funny guy, that guy, oh boy.

He say he tried to rent a car but they had no car. So he had to take a taxi from the airport and he pay two hundred dollars. Two hundred! What a big spender. But if you got it..., *tu sabes?*

Nick say he needed to stay here. I say, "*Sí, claro que sí.*" Like I say, we got plenty of room. We had a few people here because of *la tormenta.* We had your cousin Chuche and her husband, Carlos, they lost their house, and then the neighbors Ana and Felix, and your Titi Inez, and Blanca's friend Adriana. They all lost their house. Adriana, she was sleeping in her car after her apartment got flooded, and Blanca saw her and tell her to come here. "Don't sleep in the car. You can no live that way."

Oh, *y* Bobo was here, too. You remember Bobo! Blanca's baby brother. They call him that because when he was little he put a dress on a pig, and the pig no like it. He's tall, big, with crazy hair and a big beard. You remember, you used to play with him when you were a kid. He would throw you like a football until you got too chubby.

Bobo, he live by himself up in the mountains. He's like a big kid, *tu sabes*, in his head. But he build a little house all by hisself for him and his goat, and he say the house stay up in the hurricane, but he came here, with his goat, Doña Olga Tañón, to see how we doing. Once he saw everyone staying here, he say he want to stay here to keep us safe. Imagine. Anyway, he didn't stay in the house, though, he sleep on the roof every night. With the dog and Olga Tañón.

So Nick, when he came, we had a good time drinking and making jokes. We told him he can stay in the living room, and we put a pillow and blanket on the couch. But he laughed. I thought he told a joke, but I no understand. But he say, "No, no, no, I can't sleep on no couch. My back kill me." *'chacho, pobrecito hombre.* He's a hard-working man.

Qué? Oh, no, no, I don't know his job.

So, yeah, right away Ana and her husband Felix, they say, "Take our room, it's okay. We small people, we stay on the couch."

Nick, what a guy, right away he took twenty dollars and gave it to Felix, and Felix say, "No, no, 'sok."

And Nick say, "You say my money's no good? You don't want my f'ing money."

And Felix say, "No, no, no, 'sok."

And Nick, he pushed the money into Felix pants. "Take the f'ing money."

Nick, what a guy, but his mouth, oh my god. Everything is f this and f that. Well, what can you do? He's from New York.

The next day Nick say he need a car. Blanca right away she

say, "All the highways are close. You crazy, you can't go nowhere." That's how she is.

Nick say he want to take a tour. "To see what?" she say. "It all looks the same. Stay near the house. It's dangerous."

But he say he need a car, and no one can tell him no. I tell him we got the truck but it's underneath the mango tree. It fell on top, smash everything, *lo rompio todito*. I told him the only car that work here belong to Adriana.

Adriana, she's young. Very pretty. Very smart. She went to *colegio, pero* she work at El Pollo Tropical because that's all they have. Ain't no work here.

So, Nick say, "How about it? I gotta rent your car. How much you want?" He say he give her twenty dollars a day.

She say, "You want it, you gotta pay." Because she saw how Nick was with money. She say, "Fifty dollars a day."

He say she was crazy, but he was smiling.

Then she say, but she got no gasoline.

So that day we all went to the lines. Blanca to get the water. Chuche and her husband went to get food. Nick say he go with Adriana, and Bobo want to go to because everywhere Adriana go, he want to go. I went with them to get the diesel for the generator.

The line was very long and go very slow.

So Nick, he say, "Hey, Bobo, you look the f'ing same forever. They tell me you live in the mountains. You got a goat for a wife? *Ja ja ja.*"

Nick, he always making jokes, always.

No, no, Bobo say, "I don't have a wife! I would like a wife!"

"*Ja ja,*" Nick say, "you gotta get a girlfriend before you get a wife. You got a girlfriend, Bobo? Or do you just use a hole in a coconut tree?"

Ja. That Nicky. Very funny.

That line, it takes five, six hours sometimes. Nick, you could see, he no used to it. He see the guy coming back *con dos jarras de* gasoline and he told him, "I give you fifty dollars for the gas." But the guy no want it. Nick say, "Hundred dollars." The guy say, *"Que se moje los pies." Tu sabes? El que quiere pescado que se moje los pies.* Like that.

By the time we got back it was too dark to go driving. So, we tell Nick we would have a party. *Tu sabes,* not a real party, but *para celebrar* that he came to see us when things are really bad.

All we had to eat was Chef Boyardee, Spam, and rice. I told Nick I feel bad that's all we had to give him. *"Pero, cuando hay hambre, no hay pan duro."*

He say, "I don't like that can stuff. What about *cabrito*? That thing's just right there. *Cabrito's* f'ing delicious."

"Ja ja." I laughed. But Bobo, he no laugh. Right away, he took Olga Tañón and he hide her.

So we didn't have *cabrito*, but we had rum! And we had lamps all around the backyard, and Chuche started playing old records from her phone. Everything around was dark, black dark, and you see campfire and lights here and there, and you hear the *coquis* singing.

Nick, he got up and he grabbed Adriana to dance. And she had a few drinks and she was laughing. Everyone have a good time.

But then Bobo he come back from the woods, and maybe he had too much to drink. Blanca would know. Anyway, I think he want to dance, too, so he tried to get in with Adriana, but Nick no let him cut in, so Bobo took Nick's hands and started dancing with him! *Ja ja ja.* You should have seen Nick's face.

Ah, that was a nice party. We keep going until Chuche's battery die.

Anyway, the next day, Nick put the gas in the car and he go. He came back in two hours, wet from his feet to his head.

He say, "What happened to the f'ing bridge to Utuado?"

"Inequivocamente la tormenta de la bruja Maria," I say.

He say he try to swim but that *corriente* was something else.

Blanca told him, "Why you want to go to Utuado? You crazy? It's the same as here. But they got less food and more mosquitoes." That's how she is.

"I need to get across the river," he say. "You know someone who got a boat?"

I told him there was my best friend Juan Pablo, but I had not seen him since *la tormenta* when he went to go check on the boat.

Blanca she cross herself when I say Juan Pablo, and then she say, "You should ask Bobo. His old teacher lives in Utuado and he goes all the time to bring them food."

So Nick go and talk to Bobo, but no joking this time. He say, "I have to get across."

And Bobo, say, "*Como no! Vamos!*"

So they go and in two hours they come back, and Nick is wet again, his feet to his head. *Bobo, estaba todo seco.*

I say, "What happened?"

"This f'ing idiot," Nick say, "he takes me to a f'ing rope bridge, a rope bridge out a f'ing Indiana Jones movie, twenty feet about the f'ing water, three thin-for-nothing ropes, and he expects me to get across on that. So I tell him, I can't walk that f'ing thing. And you know what this motherf'er does, he picks me up like I'm a f'ing baby and starts carrying me across."

"So what happened?"

"What the f do you think happened? I'm not going to have a guy carry me like a baby? I fight him."

"He fell in the water. Splash!" Bobo say. *Ja ja ja.*

"I need a drink," Nick say. Then he tell Bobo, "One of these days I'm going to find your f'ing goat and barbecue it good and eat it. After I f it to death."

Bobo, he no think that was funny. So he walked away, into the woods. Nick, he started drinking—he finished almost all the rum we had in the house—and he use the generator to start his phone and he played music, and Adriana came by from the line with five gallons of water, and she say she need a drink. And then those two be very close, and we left them alone.

Later, after all the lights were off, Adriana came to say good-night to Blanca and me because she always did that. *Ella muy cariñosa.* She knock on the door, and we were under the mosquito net, almost sleeping. I could tell she had too much to drink. Blanca told her to come in and she did and she sat on the floor and start crying.

Blanca, her hand to her heart, she say, "*Niña, tienes que tener cuida'o.* He's a nice guy, but you know how men are."

I didn't say nothing. I know to keep quiet. Women are always right, remember.

Adriana, say, "He my only chance to get out. I got nothing. I lose everything."

And Blanca got up and she heat up some *leche evaporada* for her.

The next day, on the line for gasoline, I was with Nick and someone tell him that if he drive up this mountain road and come down, the river is small and there's a little bridge right there and the road to take you to Utuado. That made Nick happy, so the next day he went out again in Adriana's car.

And when he came back, this time he was covered in mud. Blanca no let him in the house and she gave him *un galón de agua* to clean himself outside.

He say, "I need workers. A couple of strong guys."

I told him, yeah, he could go to the gasoline line and ask people and they would help him. "*Cada cual sabe donde le aprieta el zapato.*"

"It can't just be just anybody. They can't be snitches," he say, and I say, "I'm sorry I'm too old, Felix is too skinny, Carlos is too old. But Bobo, Bobo is big and strong like ten men. Just ask Bobo."

So later he tell Bobo, "Adriana and I are going on an adventure tomorrow, and we want you to come."

So, Bobo, he like adventure. He's like a kid. So he say he go.

The next day, I get up and they left, no good morning, see you later, have a nice day. Nothing. And someone came in the night and took my tools, my shovels, *un pico, tu sabes,* a pickaxe. *Ai yi yi.* Then it started to rain. *Un aguacero.* All day. Not like *la bruja*

Maria, tu sabes, but *lluvia* and wind and *lluvia.* *'chacho,* the last thing we need.

Night come and they no come back.

Then, three in the morning, I hear banging on the door. BANG. BANG. BANG. There was Bobo, wet like a fish, and he had Adriana in his arms. He had mud all over. *Y sangre.*

I say, "Where is Nick? What happened?"

Blanca came out screaming. She got everyone awake. They got towels and bandages.

I look outside and I don't see the car. It's still raining and the wind is still *gritando.*

"What happened?" I say. "Where is Nicky?"

Bobo, he was in shock, and Adriana was out out out. Blanca gave him some coffee. And little by little he talk.

Nick said they were going on an adventure. So he drive them to Utuado to *una finca abandona'o* up there in the mountains, I think the one that used to belong to your grandmother. Blanca knows. There's nothing there but a little house, used to be.

Bobo say they came to the house and because the mud y *la lluvia,* the house, it was hanging off the side of the cliff. And with the rain and the wind, it looked like it was going to fall any second.

So Nick say he needed this suitcase that was under the house. How it get there, I don't know. It was under the floor, but the floor was dirt, and the dirt, it change to mud, and Bobo say he saw the suitcase right there, hanging under the house on the side of the cliff.

So Nick he tell Bobo, he say, "Big boy, you go over the side and get that suitcase." He say that he would pay him money. But Bobo no care about money, one way or the other. Money mean nothing to him.

But then Adriana, she tell him, "Please do it. Bobo, you have to do it."

So Bobo, he look at her and he look at Nick and he say, "Okay."

130

They put a rope around him and hang him down. The rain was coming down and the mud, he say, *"Fue como un río."* He say, "The mud was like chocolate, but it no taste like chocolate."

He reach and he reach and he grab the case.

"Pull me up!" he say. "Pull me up!"

And they pull him up, with the case. They get in the car, and Nick start to drive the car too fast. These roads here, they very small, and the mud was coming down all around. Bobo say he was scared.

Bobo say something hit the car or the car hit something. *"Como una bofeta' de Dios,"* he say. The car, it almost flew off the mountain, but Nick turn it and it spin and crash into the side, and mud and rocks came down. Down and down. Adriana, she had blood all over, and Bobo say Nick was stuck. The steering wheel move and pin him, and his legs got stuck under the steering wheel.

Nick scream at him, "You got to get me out here, you f'ing dummy."

Bobo say he can't drive, and the car was sideways.

Nick yell at him and say, "Yes, you can. You a f'ing ox. Pull me out of here. Whatever it takes."

Bobo pull and pull, but Nick, he stay stuck. Bobo keep pulling.

"You f'ing this and this," Nick tell Bobo, "you gonna tear me in half."

Then Bobo, he got an idea. Now you know Bobo, *es buena gente.* He never hurt anybody. He just no understand.

He took the shovel—my shovel!—and he push it into Nick's legs, *asi y asi*, and chop them, *aqui,* in the meat, *tu sabes?* Then he pull Nick out. He pull the top and the legs stay. But, Bobo say, "He stop screaming."

Bobo pick up Adriana in his arms, and then took half of Nick and put him over his shoulder, and then he take the legs under his arm but they drop, and then Bobo tied them together and drag the legs in the mud.

But Bobo say, "I'm sorry, Tio Luis"—he call me "tio" even

though he's Blanca's brother—he say, "It was was too hard, *muy difícil, llevandolo'*" down the mountain with the rain and with the mud. "Too much." He say he put Nick and his legs on the side of the road and covered him with banana leaves, and then he ran all the way back here with Adriana in his arms.

Ten miles in that *aguacero.*

Well, *puedes imaginar,* we had to call the ambulance and the police. There was a big mess and they went up there and they want to know what's going on and they try to find the body but with the rain and the mud they no find nothing. We didn't say what Bobo did because we no want him to get in trouble. Just in case.

La policia, they find the car and they say it empty. Except for *sangre.* They find a hundred-dollar bill in the trunk. The police come back, saying, "Who this money belong to?" and I say it must be Nick, he a big spender. They say, "You know he have a record? Do you know he was involved in drugs?"

I say, "I don't know about that, I no see him ten, fifteen years."

They say, "We check. He been coming to Puerto Rico every year, sometimes four, five times."

That was a surprise. "I don't know why he never visit. He's a good guy," I say.

Anyway, they took away the car. They never found your cousin, God have him in heaven. *La finca* is gone, it go off the mountain and into the trees and everything up there disappear.

Adriana, she decide to move to Florida. Everybody's going there now, everybody's leaving. It getting empty around here, *tu sabes?* Bobo, he move with her. She say he save her life. She say he her hero. Imagine.

Anyway, she got a nice house over there. She got a new car. They send us pictures all the time. They keep in touch. They send us a little something now and then, *tu sabes?* We got a new refrigerator, a TV set, air-conditioner in every room. I got a new truck, but I still have to get on the line for gas sometimes.

They tell Blanca and me to come to Florida. "Move here." But we can't leave, no. This is home, *tu sabes?*

Yeah, it's still hard here, *tu sabes?* Still hard. We still have to use the generator. Doña Olga Tañón is still here, shitting all over the place. But, you see, everything going to be okay, *si Dios lo permite. Right?* And your Titi Blanca, she can make cake anytime now for you.

So when are you coming to visit?

OLD PENDEJO

Not too long ago, I hated that dog with all my heart.

I was just back from the war, about two months, still feeling like I was cleaning sand out of my ass. I had come home with a bum ear, a bum leg, and the shakes. All in all, I was feeling pretty useless. Especially to my family. We were in a tight spot, with our tiny sheep ranch that had but two sheep. Dad was long gone, my brother Jorge was deep into the meth, my sister had married off, was living back in Mexico. Ma tried to hold our family together. She kept saying the sun always had to shine again sometime. But I could see in her eyes that things looked bad even to her.

The dog just showed up one day, probably looking for scraps. I saw my brother out front, playing tug-of-war with it with an old rope.

I told him, "Jorge, get that *pinche* dog outta here before it gives you rabies."

"It's a great dog," he said, but I could see it was nothing but a rangy mutt, big bald patches of skin on it. Maybe its great grandma was a border collie, maybe, but the apple had fallen far from the tree.

"It's a mangy dog," I said. "It's gonna bring fleas into the house."

"Could be a great sheep dog," he said.

"We ain't got but two sheep, brainless," I said, but he ignored me. Didn't matter. I figured the dog would figure out there wasn't any pet chow here soon enough and then it would move along to the next sucker.

I limped to the truck and drove out to the edge of our property. Did a perimeter patrol. We lived outside of Mason, in Texas Hill country. Really pretty land. At least it used to be. You could go fly fishing one day, count wildflowers the whole next day. Now most of it was dry, unkind, not pretty. Can't keep up good land without good workers.

It was only a little while before the bank would come take it anyway, pretty or not.

The stupid dog would move on, sure enough, I thought. We didn't need another belly to disappoint.

Next morning the *pinche* dog was still around, sitting on the steps back of the kitchen door, ears up like it was expecting something. I walked over, and it scooted out of my way, its curled-up tail between its legs. But it didn't have that look that most dogs do when they're letting you know you're master. Its body was wiggling, but that dog still had this sparkly look in its eye, like it was playing me for a fool. I didn't like that. I gave it a good kick off the steps.

But I hit it with my bad leg. Dang. Bolt of pain ran up my knee and to my skull. I caught my breath, limped to the barn, and yanked the door wide open. I hollered at Jorge, "What's that moth-eaten mutt still doing 'round here?"

Jorge hit 'bout as high as the ceiling when I came in. "Marco!" The meth'll make you jumpy. "Marco! Good morning!"

He was pacing around, then he sat down, rocked from side to side, then got up and paced again.

"Don't be feeding that damn dog, *guey*," I told him, "or it'll never leave."

Then that boy did something he'd been doing a lot of lately: Bawling, rivers of tears.

"Please, Marco. I ain't got nothing here. My girl left me and took my kids. And Speedy's run off."

Speedy was our collie. Now Speedy, she had been a beauty. Smart dog. Good sheep dog. She went for a long walk months ago and hadn't come back. Very smart dog, I tell you what.

I could see the skin of Jorge's face was dry and scratched. His cheeks were already concaving from whatever the meth did to you.

"Listen. Listen," he said, getting up and then sitting back down. "I didn't get to go to school. I didn't get to go to the army. That's all you. On top of that, you're Mom's favorite. She looks at me like I'm another piece of furniture. So let me keep the stupid dog!"

My brother never was one to make a whole lot of sense. But I figured he was saying the dog made him happy. At least it wasn't going to kill him, like the meth.

"Fine," I said. "Keep the stupid dog. That's all we need."

Jorge didn't show for supper that night. Afterward, Mom and me sat in the living room, watching the news. She had her after-dinner bourbon next to her and was doing her knitting. The TV said Los Angeles was under martial law. Something about the flu getting out of hand, not enough inoculations. You hear the same thing every winter.

Mom looked up from the TV and said to me, "How you like that supper, son?"

She'd made *ropa vieja* and refried beans. It was pretty darned good. A world better than rations.

"It's great, Mom. Just like you always make it."

"Well, that just about finished that last groceries we had. You'll have to go to market end of this week."

"How's our credit?"

"We're still in good graces, *gracias a dios*," she said and knocked on the wood of her chair.

Then she handed her glass to me. "Top me off, *por favor.*"

I got up, got her bourbon, and refilled her glass. Then I finished up my supper. In New York City, they declared a state of emergency.

I had the dream again. We had just got ourselves out of a bag of dicks. We were booking away from this village, making good time in a haze of sand and dust. I was sitting in the back of a recon, watching the village shrink away. That's when we must have hit it. An explosion so loud it was the last thing my left ear would ever hear. I went tumbling, feeling things break in my body. I was on the side of the road, one arm curled under me, my other hand opening and closing on the dirt.

I woke up in the corner of my room, blankets tangled around my leg, covered with enough sweat to soak my shirt and shorts.

Lord, I hated that dream.

Well, it was about time to wake up anyway.

I hobbled downstairs and found my brother curled around that dog on the couch. You could see the ribs easy on both of them. I went to wake Jorge, when the dog bared its teeth and me and growled at me. That son of a bitch.

"Wake up, *guey!*" I said, bouncing then tilting the sunken cushions with my good foot so the danged mutt and my brother rolled off the couch and hit the floor. "Time to go to market."

Waiting in the truck, I saw Jorge was bringing the dog along, helping it into the back.

I waited till Jorge was in the truck.

"I bet you named him already?" I said.

"That I did," Jorge said, drumming on the dash like it was a conga.

"So what you name him?"

"Pendejo," he said.

"Pendejo." I laughed. "What the hell for?"

"It's the only thing he answers to. "Get out here, Pendejo!' 'Sit, Pendejo.' 'Fetch, Pendejo.' 'Old Pendejo' is his full name."

The dog was wagging its tail at us, like it knew we were talking about him. There was almost an eat-shit grin on its face. Pendejo was not a nice thing to call someone, even a dirty-looking, curly-haired, mangy dog. But I guess the name kind of fit.

When we pulled into the Super S mart, there were a mess of cars and trucks parked outside. People were coming out with two or three shopping carts apiece, hauling away food, water, supplies.

We passed Mr. Perez loading the back of his 4x4.

"Morning, Mr. Perez," we both said.

"Marco. Jorge. Seems like new deliveries didn't come this week and won't be coming next week. Better stock up now, boys."

We said our thanks, found a parking spot, and went inside the store. The dog would've followed us—it wanted to be wherever Jorge was—but my brother got some rope and tied it up in our truck bed.

I hadn't seen this kind of chaos in the store since the last round of big tornadoes we had a few years back. The shelves were near bare, and there was no beer left at all.

We were just about finished loading the back of the truck, the damn pooch Pendejo watching us the whole time, wagging its smartass tail. It had chewed through the thick rope Jorge had tied it up with. Some chops on that dog.

Jorge went up front to start the truck. That's when I heard him yell.

I looked around the side and saw one guy punch my brother square in the face, knocking him back, then pull him out of the cab. Another guy right was behind that guy with a crowbar. It was the Diaz brothers, Ty and Brandon. Local roughhouses. I

139

went to move, but the pain that shot through my leg stuck me in place.

That's when the dog jumped them. It had gotten to the roof of the cab without my seeing, and from there it landed right into Ty's chest with its paws, pushing him back and away from Jorge. Brandon took a step toward him with the bar, but Old Pendejo flashed its teeth and growled like a bear and stood its ground. Jorge lay twitching on the ground, dazed and bloody.

Brandon swung the crowbar, but the dog was faster, and leaped high and bit the air—so close to Brandon's face he must have felt the breeze.

"Whoa! Villalobos. Back your dog off," Brandon said. "Thing's probably got rabies."

"What you want, Brandon?"

"We just want the truck, Marco. Just give us the truck."

"Get your own goddamn truck."

"Ours broke down. We gotta get gone out of town."

"I ain't letting you. And sure enough this pooch ain't letting you."

"Hell with this," Brandon said, and he dragged his brother up and they got out of there. Pendejo kept up his barking and growling the whole time till they were out of sight.

I helped my brother up, and we both got the dog into the cab. Then I hit the gas.

If we'd had to go toe to toe with the Diaz boys, well, it wouldn't've been hard, but it wouldn't've been easy, what with my leg and all. I had to admit the dog impressed me, I tell you what.

"That Old Pendejo's full of fight," my brother said, beating the conga again on the dash. "And you wanted to get rid of him."

"Good boy, Old Pendejo. Good boy."

We both laughed. It was good to laugh with my brother again.

* * *

On the way back to the house, Mom called my cell and told me she'd gone over to Mrs. Coleman's, who'd taken ill. Mrs. Coleman had two daughters, both of whom had moved to the coasts soon as they were old enough, so she had no one to take care of her. Mom was always doing stuff like that for people.

It was before noon, and my brother said he didn't feel like looking over two scrawny sheep. I guess his laziness was catching because I didn't feel like doing much of anything either. Maybe it was because my knee was throbbing. Maybe it was because Mom wasn't around for the first time in a long time, and so it felt like we were kids who had the run of the house.

I said to my brother, "You want a beer, Jorge?"

"Say what? It's not even noon, bro."

"I'm getting a beer."

"Hell, then get me one, too."

So we sat drinking beers in the living room, me in Pop's old chair, and Jorge in Mom's, and Old Pendejo cleaning hisself on the rug in front of us, making these disgusting licking sounds.

"I wish I could do that," Jorge said.

"Don't you think you should get to know the dog a little more, *guey*," I said, and we both got a kick out of that for a while.

Jorge broke into a bag of chips and ate them like a starving man. "Chips," he said. "Chiiippps," between and during bites.

After a few beers I told him I was worried about Mom.

"She'll be all right. Mrs. Coleman still has her old shotgun she used to scare us with as kids."

"No, I mean, Mom, Mom's getting older, and this ranch ain't got the legs to go much longer."

"It's pretty much past dead, you ask me."

I looked at him. His body seemed melted right into the chair. He looked even more useless than I felt.

"I'm worried about you too, Jorge."

He laughed. "You got your own problems. Let mine be mine."

We didn't say nothing for the longest time after that. Just drank beer after beer. The TV was on, but there was no picture and no sound.

"Cable's out," my brother said. "Shoot, it was just on last night. Something about air traffic being stopped, borders being closed."

"Same old drill," I said.

"Same old drill," he said.

I cracked open another beer. My brother kept shifting around in his chair, kind of restless, picking and scratching at hisself. Sometimes he would get up and walk around the room, and the dog would follow him. Finally, Jorge put in a DVD for some action movie we'd seen a million times. But then he started talking.

"What was up with those Diaz brothers today?" he said, looking at the screen.

"Just loco," I told him. "They were always a few sandwiches short of a picnic."

He laughed. "But why would they want to leave town? You think this virus from the news got them spooked?"

"Everything spooks them. Here we are, miles from the nearest big town. We got nothing to worry about. Worst thing'll happen, it'll hit Houston. They'll make people wash their hands a lot, and that'll be the end of it," I said.

"But, Marco, I heard—I heard that people that pass from this thing...well, they don't stay dead."

I about spit up my beer. "That's ridiculous, bro."

"Well, that's what I read."

"Read where?"

"On the Internet. Though it's not working."

"What you mean?"

"I don't know. Internet went down last night. Probably 'cause of the cable."

"People spend too much time on the Internet anyway," I said. "That's all fake news and commercials. Shoulda seen all the stuff they wrote about us in Iraq. Don't pay that garbage any mind."

It was getting on long past suppertime, and we'd finished three six packs. I looked over at Jorge, and he was looking kind of paler than normal.

"You look tuckered out, *guey*. Go on to your room and get some rest," I told him.

He said maybe I was right and took off. The dog followed right behind him. Me, I took two steps and collapsed onto the couch. I propped my bum leg on a pillow and fell out.

When I woke up, it was nighttime. I rolled over and saw my wallet on the floor. Must've fallen out when I fell asleep. It was empty.

I found the dog tied to the front porch and gnawing on the thick piece of rope keeping him there.

My brother had lit out.

I had an idea where Jorge was, out at the abandoned Cactus Motel. Kids been getting high there for years. Even I used to go there when I was young and had nothing to do. I got out my M9 pistol from my footlocker, loaded it. I pictured aiming it right at Jorge's head. I should go get him and drag his ass back home. *Pinche guey.*

But who did I think I was? I couldn't save him. I wasn't good for anything. I put the gun in the drawer next to my bed and threw myself down on the mattress.

That night the dream came back.

We were stabilizing that village, going from door to door, crossing out unfriendlies. Young and old, innocent and guilty. Didn't matter. Yes, sir, right away, sir. We booked out of there, making good time in a cloud of sand and dust. I was sitting in the back of a truck, watching the village shrink away, looking at the blood covering my boots. Then came the explosion so loud. I went tumbling, feeling things break in my body. On the side of the road, I had one arm curled under me, my other hand opening and closing on the dirt. Then someone was calling my name, getting my attention, bringing me back to consciousness. "Villalobos! Villalobos! You all right?" It was my CO, and I think he saved my life, snapping me awake before I could fall deeper into the kind of complete oblivion you don't wake up from.

I fell on the floor again, blankets around my leg, covered with sweat. I dragged myself up.

I noticed then the dog was in the room. He walked slowly over to me, his dirty nails scratching on the floor, wagging his dirty tail, and damn if that dog didn't sit down right in front of me and put his head in my lap. He looked up at me with these huge brown eyes. Looking right through me.

I got up, got myself a shot from my bottle next to my bed, sat back down in that spot on the floor, and the dog put his head right back where it was before, and looked up at me with big brown eyes full of pity.

I woke up late, a few hours past dawn, and I was about to call Mom on my cell, when the house phone rang.

"Marco. *Gracias a dios!* Hurry!"

When your mother calls you half-hysterical on the phone, you better get going. I didn't think twice when the dog followed me into the truck, and we raced out the ranch in a cloud of dust.

I heard what sounded like a shotgun blast echo over the hills.

The truck had good pickup, and I floored it.

The dog and I jumped out of the car at the same time and ran for the door, Old Pendejo barking fiercely the whole way. I ripped open the front door. He pushed right past my legs and ran inside. In the foyer it smelled like a thousand places I knew in the war. In the kitchen, there was Mom sitting on the floor, a shotgun in her lap.

And there, in front of her on the floor, was Mrs. Coleman.

With her head busted open like a pumpkin tossed out a speeding truck. I'd see things like that before, but seeing it on Mrs. Coleman's plain, brown kitchen floor just made it much more disgusting. She had on her bunny slippers, too.

My mom started talking. "She got the strangest fever I ever saw," Mom said. "She was so cold, so cold. I made her some soup, but she wouldn't eat it. Did you boys eat?"

"Yes, Mom, we ate."

Mom nodded. Her hair, which was always neatly combed, was a big cotton candy mess above her head. There was blood all over her apron.

"What happened, Mom?"

"She got up, looking horrible. Really bad. And then she attacked me. Like she was...like she was trying to eat me. She was trying to eat me! She clawed me like an animal!"

My mother showed me long, deep scratches on her arm.

"I got to get you to the hospital."

"I shot her. You have to understand, I had to. Then she got up again. She got up again. So I had to shoot her again."

I saw then that Mrs. Coleman also had a spread of gunshot across her left side. No sixty-year-old lady would've been able to withstand one blast, let alone two.

"I'll call the sheriff later," I said.

Mom showed me the cell phone in her hand. "I tried. No answer."

She seemed like she was in shock, but she said she just wanted to go home. I picked her up and carried her to the truck.

She whispered, "Drive fast, Marquito."

I wanted to get Jorge, but Mom was sick, and I had to take care of her. I sat on the floor right outside her room while she slept. Old Pendejo, he stayed right there with me.

I went downstairs and made some toast and tea with a little of her bourbon and brought it up to her. The dog came into the

145

room with me.

"Some food for you, Mom."

She was propped up on a bunch of pillows and staring out at nothing. It looked like she had a fever, but she felt cold, was pale as hell.

"Thank you, son. But I don't think I could keep it down."

"Well, I'll just put it here. Tea's got some bourbon in it."

She reached for that right away. She said, "I see that mangy dog is still around."

"Yeah, he's Jorge's. Pendejo's his best friend," I said and sat down in the chair by her bed. The dog sat on the floor next to me, and my hand naturally went to pet him.

"Looks like he's pretty attached to you, too."

"I guess."

Mom suffered a lot in her life. My dad was from Mexico City, and he met Mom when he was in the army back in the day. She was from Fajardo, which is in Puerto Rico. That's right, we're Mexiricans. Mom used to live right on the beach, she told us. But Dad took her deep into the dusty heart of Texas, I guess, where the skies go on blue forever, but there ain't no beaches in sight. I know she had a tough life here on the ranch, with one son a druggie and the other pretty much a gimp.

But what on Earth could have made her shoot Mrs. Coleman in the head? Mom was too young to be senile, wasn't she?

"Where's that wonderful brother of yours anyway?" she said.

"He's—." I couldn't think of a lie fast enough.

"I know. You don't have to tell me."

I didn't say nothing. I just kept petting the dog.

She said, "He's why I hide my money all over the house, you know."

"I know."

She finished the tea and put down the cup. "I gotta close my eyes for a few minutes. You don't have to stay."

* * *

146

I closed the door behind me and stood there in the hallway, feeling more useless than ever.

That's when the dog started wagging its tail. Touching my hand with its nose and then going to the stairs and coming back to do it again.

"What's the matter, boy? What's the matter, Pendejo?"

The dog led me outside, and then he did the damnedest thing. He found this rope and he nudged it right up to me. I picked up one end and right away he picks up the other in his teeth.

Dang. My brother was out getting high, and my mother had just killed her friend and now was upstairs sick with Lord knows what, and all this stupid dog wanted to do was play tug-of-war.

Stupid simple-ass animal.

And you know what?

With the heat of sundown on my shoulders, and Old Pendejo pulling so hard I could feel an ache in my forearms, I felt like a kid again, like a boy, better than I had felt in years.

It was a good feeling.

Stupid dog. Right there he taught me something important. Enjoy the little things, the small moments.

And then he stopped.

He dropped the rope from his mouth and turned toward the western arm of the ranch, where a series of hills lead over to the Coleman property.

There were three of them coming over the hill. With the sun behind them I couldn't see their faces. They walked slowly, wobbly, like they had all the time in the day and more to burn.

The dog started barking, then running toward them, and then running back, behind me. The dog was scared. I thought this dog had the biggest *cojones* I'd ever seen. But now he was scared and tucked behind me.

I looked back at the three figures. I was about to call out, when right then another figure ran out from a small grove of trees we had, over to my left.

It was Jorge, his mouth opening and closing, yelling something. I could hear it like a whisper in my left ear. It took a second to work it out.

"Marco! Marco! Run!"

The dog ran to him, jumping up and down on him, barking. Jorge ignored him.

"Get your guns, bro!"

The three figures weren't much closer. But I could see they looked pretty odd. One looked like it had a broken neck.

There was a Remington 700 in the house, and the M9. I hobbled back into the house and grabbed the rifle.

"What's going on?" I yelled at my brother, who was coming up the stairs behind me.

"Give me the rifle," he yelled back.

"You're getting the gun."

"Why not the rifle?"

In my room, I checked the pistol, then handed it to my brother.

"Why can't I get the rifle?" he said. "I have to get up close with this!"

I ignored him and checked out the window and the three figures were just approaching the front yard. Then I realized there were a few more a few yards behind them. I could see now that there was something wrong with all of them. They were deadly pale, some of them had blood all over their mouths. One of them for sure had a broken neck. Another had a kitchen knife in its chest.

"Who the hell are these people?" I said.

"They came to the Cactus," he said. "At first I couldn't tell them apart from everybody else. And then they just started eating people. It's that virus, I tell you, that virus!"

"Whatever," I said. "*Vamos.*"

You live in the Texas Hill country like we do, with its small towns and big ranches, its oaks and its rivers, and the miles of big open sky, you sometimes forget there is a whole other world out there. You think the world out there can't touch you. Sometimes you forget. Until you're forced to face it.

As I stepped out the door I shot the first one. The bullet went through his chest and he kept coming. Next shot I stood my ground and aimed. Right between the eyes. He went down.

My brother took aim and shot the ground in front of another one.

"Aim for the chest," I yelled.

He did and shot the next one right in the face.

"Again," I said.

Old Pendejo didn't have a gun but he was barking his face off. He looked nervous, ready to pounce, standing there between me and my brother. Good dog.

We had four of them down by the time I had to reload. I could smell them from the front steps. It was a nasty, hot smell, like being upwind of a body dump next to an overused latrine.

Just as I was reloading, that smell got even more powerful. Coming from my right. Just as I turned, I felt the dog right behind me. I saw him crashing into two of them.

Before I could react, I saw another one come out the trees, stumbling. I took a breath and aimed and breathed out and shot. His head split open.

I heard the dog howl. Old Pendejo was ripping and pulling at one thing but the other one was clawing, and sinking its teeth into the poor dog's hide.

I fired the rifled but it was empty. So I used it like a bat, swinging and knocking the biter's head up and cocked to the side. With two more swings I had crushed its skull. The dog meanwhile had made quick work of the other one.

"That's teamwork, boy," I said. And Pendejo, his muzzle covered in blood, barked back.

"We got those," my brother said. He was pale and scratched up.

"You look like hell," I told him.

"I'm still prettier than you," he said.

"*Pinche guey.*"

"Listen, man, we gotta get outta here. There's more of them coming."

"What are those things?"

He asked where Mom was, and I told her she was upstairs, sick.

"Sick with what?"

I told him about what I'd seen at Mrs. Coleman's, that I'd thought Mom had maybe snapped and killed our old neighbor. But now that I'd seen these things, I didn't know.

My brother right there checked his weapon for ammo. "Marco, listen, we gotta...we gotta take care of her."

"Of course, *guey*—"

"No, we can't let the old lady go that way."

"What do you mean?"

"The virus. She's probably got the *pinche* virus. She's gonna turn into one of them."

"Hold on," I said, but he was running up the stairs. The dog took a look at me and ran after him. "Jorge! Wait!"

Running up the stairs was not an option for me. But I couldn't let Jorge do what he was going to do. I took the steps fast as I could, pulling myself up. He was right at her door.

"Jorge, stop!"

Then he was in Mom's room. I forced myself the rest of the way, got to her door. He was aiming at her. "Jorge." He turned. I stood my ground and aimed. And shot.

He crumpled to the floor, a single hole in his head.

I could hear Old Pendejo whimpering on the landing.

I bent down to check my brother, putting the gun down— and from behind me my mother latched on to my neck.

She was one of them now. Jorge had been right. She'd been infected.

She was skinny as a stalk of wheat but strong.

I clawed around for the pistol on the floor. And then I used it.

The house was quiet after that. I didn't feel anything. The world had turned into a crazier place that I ever could've imagined. I had fought a war to help protect my people, the people I loved—and I had just killed them.

I checked the MP. One bullet left.

Old Pendejo whimpered some more. He nudged me in my leg, but gently, almost caressing it. That's when I realized. He was all bit up, too, like Mom had been. And those crazies outside.

Could it turn a dog? I wonder if he was wondering that, too.

He looked at me with those big, brown blazing eyes. He knew. And he knew what I had to do.

I had seen some of my best friends killed in front of me, but I never did for them what I did for that dog. I stuck the muzzle of the gun against his hide and pulled the trigger. He was a good dog. A damn good dog.

"Goodbye, Pendejo," I said.

Wasn't much gas left but I figured I'd take the truck as far as it would go.

I got a few miles from the house when I saw them. Over two dozen of them, moving on the road that slow, stumbly way they do. There was no way around them. I revved the engine. As I came to them, they looked up and reached out for me.

I plowed. They were softer than people.

They flew apart in pieces.

There were so many of them.

I lost control of the truck. I couldn't see where I was going with the blood on the windshield. The engine lurched. Then I hit something. Hard. The truck spun and turned, and turned over. Glass. Metal crunching. Then it stopped.

I crawled halfway out, got to my feet, reached back, trembling, for the rifle.

They were coming for me.

I got partway to my knees and took a position. I started shooting at everything that moved, my rage boiling in my guts.

"Pinche gringo culero ve a chingar a tu reputisima madre!"

I shot and reloaded, shot and reloaded.

"Pinche gringo culero ve a chingar a tu reputisima madre!"

And then—I thought there would be more. But it was silent there on the road.

I collapsed on the ground. Something else was broken inside me.

I couldn't get very far. I didn't have the will. I didn't want to go no more. I was on the side of the road. I had one arm curled under me, my other hand opening and closing on the dirt.

It took a long while, but then he came. Of course he would. I turned my head as much as I could and saw him, walking slowly in. Doing that death walk, but on four legs. He looked even mangier. Old Pendejo. Bullet hole in his side. Those old sparkling eyes empty now, but still looking right at me.

Well. If it's going to happen, might as well be your best friend.

I could feel the old boy's hot breath on my neck—it stank like the dead, stank like that tiny village I walked out of long ago—and just as a drop of foamy spittle hit me and made me shiver, my dog bit.

LA VOLCANA

Juniper Jiminez should've been thinking about the robbery taking place below her, should've been planning strategy, ensuring public safety. But instead she thought about new boots, a bubble bath, a manicure, Javier. And of course, she needed to visit her mother because she hadn't gone in days and Juniper couldn't understand why she didn't just go. But she couldn't do any of those things at the moment.

Because Juniper was a superhero whose *nom de guerre* was La Volcana (aka the Chica of Charcoal, aka the Mami of Magma)— and she had a job to do.

So she stayed where she was—floating on a cushion of superheated air just atop a column of fire, twenty-five feet above the ground. She was waiting for her arch-nemesis Aqua-Bella and her gang to emerge from the First National Bank. They were taking such a long time that Juniper considered melting the windows to get the whole thing over with.

"Hey, criminals," she said, resisting the urge to check her phone to see if Javier had texted back. "C'mon, come out with your hands up already."

With a splash, Aqua-Bella emerged through the doors, in her shimmering, opalescent costume, her matching henchpersons, the Diving Bells, close behind. She looked up and dramatically

153

proclaimed, "I knew you'd be here!"

Juniper raised her hands to create a cage of flame around them. "Your MO is as transparent as your face. I..."

Cutting off her words was something that came on like a migraine, starting in the middle of her forehead, then cleaving the back of her skull. The cage dissipated. The column of fire vanished.

The Femme of Fire fell, denting the roof of a parked car with a WHOOMP.

Aqua-Bella shouted to her cohorts, "Skeddaddle!" and they piled into a getaway van like azure-clad clowns.

Dazed, La Volcana sat up. Her head throbbed, her spine felt out of alignment. She attempted to shoot a ball of fire at the van, but all that came out from her fingers was a puff of sulphurous smoke. She slumped back on the hood.

When the police arrived, she was vomiting in the street.

"Yet another reason to call you La Volcana." This from Detective Sergeant Hector Hostos. Her husband. His hair was perfectly sculpted, his eyebrows perfectly trimmed.

She cursed him, but through the bile it came out as "Fffrughhdgu."

He bent down to whisper to her, "What the hell happened?

"C-couldn't stop her."

"What do you mean? She's just an animated puddle. You could have turned her into a facial."

"Ass! My powers...stopped."

"What? No. Oh no! You're not pregnant, are you? Tell me you're not pregnant."

"You know that's not it. My powers shut off. Don't know why."

"Well, shit."

"Thanks for the TLC," she said, trying to straighten up. Everyone had a camera now. She had to look professional.

"We'll talk about it tonight," Hector said, walking into the bank. "We have a lot to discuss."

154

"Yeah," she said. "Sure we do."

Juniper had a cab drop her off a mile from the secret entrance to her base. She balked at the amount of the fare, but what could she do? One complaint and she'd be crucified on social media. "La Volcana got all stingy in my cab. Who she think she is? Screw her!!"

She slid down the long chute that she normally flew into. From her secret base, she walked another half mile to the home she shared with Hector, and once inside, she threw off her clothes, except for bra, underwear, and socks.

On her knees, she dug into the couch cushions for the pack of cigarettes stashed there. She put a menthol in her mouth and then pointed a finger at the tip. Nothing. She snapped her fingers, just as she did when her mother first taught her to generate sparks as a toddler. Still nothing. She stomped around in search for matches but then realized there were none in the house. "Oh fuck me!"

She forced herself up and realized, duh, she now had time for that bubble bath she had been dreaming of. She made the water hot by turning on the hot water, which was new to her, and she watched the bubbles multiply before sinking herself into it. But she couldn't even light the goddamn scented candles.

A damp towel over her eyes, she said, aloud, "So what the hell was that about?"

She remembered how her mama, the famous Lady Lava, showed her how to make her own lunch by placing two slices of buttered bread in her palms with some cheese. Her mother held her hands over her daughter's, heating them until they felt on fire She screeched but her mother said, "The pain in just in your mind, sweetheart, just in your mind," and then seconds later opened her hands, saying "Voila!" And there was a sandwich with perfectly melted cheese and grill marks shaped like her eight-year-old palms.

They would come back, her powers. She just needed time off, time to relax, time to listen only to her own breathing.

So she breathed. And breathed some more.

She was surprised when the water started to cool. "Oh, yeah," she said, and as she went to turn the tap again, the phone rang. She jumped out of the tub, slipping and bumping her knee on the edge. "Damn! Fuck!"

"Hey, Junie!"

It was Nikki Norwood, alias Sonic Sistah. She'd just gone through a difficult divorce from her husband Harold (alias Sonic Soljah). The big issue had been not only custody of SS-T and Sonic Kimberlee, but also of the Sonic formula and brand. Harold had dreamed up the serum, but Nikki had made it work, and had turned them into a viable team. The judge took her side, but Harold was appealing the decision.

"Oh, it's you, Nikki."

"Don't sound so happy about it."

"Sorry. Rough day."

"I heard. Tough luck with Bella today. What was that about?"

"Oh, just a bad day on the job."

"Please. I hear you."

Nikki was tough herself—and she could sing notes high enough to shatter concrete. But Juniper knew her friend overreacted to everything, so she didn't mention the loss of her powers. Instead, she said, "I think I need a new costume. I look so fat in this one."

"You fat?! My right thigh, after a month on the keto diet, is still fatter than you. Please. I'm the one who needs a new costume. But can I afford it? No. Crimefighting does not pay. Unless you get a talk show like Dr. Mentallo or turn gigolo like the LatinX Fly."

Juniper laughed nervously. "I just got a new costume, and it doesn't fit quite right. Do you know how much fireproof boots cost? Oh my god!"

"Please. I'm the one who needs to do something new. I feel

like yesterday's news in this town."

"You're doing fine, Nikki," Juniper said, pulling out a cigarette and walking quickly to the stove before she realized they hadn't had gas in the stove for years.

"Hey, the girls are all going patrolling together tonight. Why don't you come with? It's always fun when we get together."

"Uh, no, sorry, Nikki. I have to go visit Mom."

"Oh, all right. Right. Give her my best then."

For the rest of the afternoon, Juniper did the laundry and checked her phone only three more times.

An hour before Hector was due home, she took a train back to the city.

In her crimson costume, with its cowl and fiery mask and the bright purple V that stretched from her cleavage to her bellybutton, she was constantly ogled, constantly catcalled. But now, walking around in civvies, she was anonymous. No a single whistle. For which she was grateful.

She was able to get a slice of brick-oven pizza without hearing any wisecracks. She witnessed a pickpocketing, but the victim, too drunk to notice, was waddling into a strip club, so she said nothing. A few blocks on, she heard a domestic disturbance: two women yelling at each other in a first-story apartment. After a minute, Juniper realized they were arguing about a TV show.

Then she turned a corner and saw the fire.

It was raging in a tenement in the middle of a block lined with identical brownstones. Three fire trucks, firemen running back and forth, a ladder being hoisted, the smell of burning plastic. A father and a little girl were crying in a heap by the curb. Juniper stood across the stream and watched the flames lick at the window tops and stream out of a hole in the roof. They were bright, gorgeous, hungry flames. If she had her powers, she could have breathed them in and saved the day. But they had things under control. They didn't need her, and that made her smile.

She made her way to the waterfront. The area was once a hub of criminal activity, but in recent years had become gentrified. Warehouses converted to lofts, cheap diners transformed into pricey bistros. But right by the shore one little bar resisted change—Tim Riley's Bar & Grille, a well-worn, smoked-filled pub lined with an atmosphere that only time, nicotine, and loyalty could create. It was and remained a supervillain hangout.

Inside, cigarette and cigar smoke stung her eyes, but she could see the place was crowded and she recognized quite a few of the crowd. Right by the door was Stretch Sanchez, an asshole who used his powers to assault women blocks away. Bastard. If she had her powers, she'd roast him like a frank right there, screw the law. He was listening to the Blue Streak, who sat next to the She-Bulk. Over in a dark corner was the Sword, a superhero. This would have been a surprise, but he was swapping spit with the Velvet Glove, his archenemy. Everyone knew they had been knocking boots for years.

Juniper walked all the way to the bathrooms and back to the front.

Nope, Javier wasn't there.

She took a seat at the bar and ordered a vodka and tonic from the bartender, a woman she recognized as the Demoness. The horns in her head needed a trimming, buffing, and polish.

She was halfway into her second drink, listening to the R&B jukebox and letting a light buzz from the cocktail curl her toes, when she heard a familiar voice. She turned around and saw, through the dim light, alone in a booth: Aqua-Bella. Cackling to herself.

Juniper didn't know what motivated her to do what she did next. Maybe morbid curiosity. Maybe plain stupidity.

She took her drink and went over.

Aqua-Bella was holding an empty red cigarette holder in her mouth. The red reflected in her shimmering watery face.

"Run out of cigarettes?" Juniper said.

"This?" Bella said, holding the holder in her fingers. "I

smoked like a chimney when I was young. But ever since I got my water abilities, I don't dare. Dehydrates me too much. So does the liquor, but if I have to choose between the two I'm going to have my little drinks. A liquid lunch for a liquid lady!"

This struck Juniper as hilarious, and both women laughed.

"What's your name, sweetheart?"

"Samantha," Juniper said.

"That's pretty. Here, scoot over and let Roger sit."

Juniper looked up and there was a man there with a large tumbler of whiskey and a bottle of beer.

"I'm Bella. This is Roger. Roger, this is Sam, my new friend."

Roger was a short, fat man with bucked teeth and red cheeks. He smelled of onion rings and antibacterial soap.

"Are you a super-human?" he asked her.

"No, no. But I make a super omelet!" she said. It was one of Hector's old jokes, and she felt a little guilty using it.

"Me, too. A normal human, I mean," said Roger. "Aqua here is the star."

"Oh, Roger." Aqua-Bella took large sips from the tumbler. It gave her a brown tint. "Old me, a star. I'm fifty-seven—today. Well, last night."

"Happy birthday!" said Juniper, struck by the coincidence that her mother had turned fifty-seven a month before.

"Thank you both." She hiccupped. "You know, Sam, Roger and I go way back. From when I wanted to be a superhero."

"A superhero?"

"Yes, I tried to be good at first." Bella and Roger laughed at that and clinked their glasses. "Well, I was an actress then. I thought it might get me a movie or a series."

"A clothing line. Action figures," said Roger.

"The whole kit and kaboodle," said Bella. "Understand—my husband was long gone, living in Europe with his sister. Long story. Won't bore you."

Juniper smiled at this. She realized this was already the

longest conversation they had ever had.

"I had two children on my hands. Spoiled rotten. They needed everything."

"Christopher's braces," said Roger. "Tanya's ballet."

"And I'd just had this confounded accident that turned me into a walking bathtub without the tub. The doctor's bills were epic. So, I decided to go fight the never-ending battle, do justice! For monetary reward, mind you. Bounty hunting and all that."

Juniper had never known this. "So what happened?"

"Well, I was miserable at it. One bail jumper literally jumped right through me." Bella laughed, and Juniper noticed that when she did her whole body rippled like a pond after a stone is thrown in.

"After a few months of that," Bella said, "I didn't have much choice. I'd lost my house. Christopher was in jail. Another story. Tell it later. And then some friends of Roger came to talk to me. They said I could easily sneak in through the security system of this jewelry store. They said I had nothing to worry about."

An odd mix of feelings fluttered in Juniper's chest then—she knew where this story was going.

"And then La Volcana showed up," Roger said.

"La Volcana!" Bella said. "Caught me red-handed. What was I going to do, get turned into tea? Next morning I was in the papers. The front page! Finally! Ta da! So—my destiny was set."

"Criminal mastermind," said Roger. "Archvillainess."

Juniper remembered. It had been one of her first solo victories, important for her stepping out of her mother's shadow. "You had a choice, though," she said. "I mean, to reform."

"Reform! You are young. I know how hard it is to change your stripes once they've been set for you. It's impossible. Wait. Stripes. I made a prison pun."

Roger laughed, staring at Bella with admiration.

Juniper couldn't help feeling the same way. "You, your life is…is—"

"The word you're looking for, my dear, is pathetic," said

160

Bella. "I've never made more than a couple grand at one time. I might have done better in dinner theater. My son, Chris—my boy—he died in prison while I was in a plastic container halfway across the country. I didn't find out till a year after it happened. My daughter, my beautiful daughter, married one of my Bells. I had trusted him, on many jobs, with my life. But he's a brute and I knew it. But Tanya is in love. What can you say to your flesh and blood?"

"To flesh and blood," said Roger, raising his drink.

"Flesh and blood," said Juniper.

When she got home at two in the morning, Juniper expected Hector to be waiting at the door, screaming at her before it opened. But instead he was on the couch, having cocoa.

"I've been trying your cell phone for hours," he said. He stood up in his silk pajamas and robe.

"Isshut tit off," she said, quite drunk.

"So where have you been?"

"Patrol."

"Without your costume? And where?" He sniffed. "In a vat of booze?"

"S-s-sometimes I...withoutit."

"You can't do that. You have an image and an obligation to uphold. You can't go out and make a fool of yourself. What if you lost control? You'll endanger everything we have."

If he was talking about her going crazy with her powers while drunk, he must have forgotten that she'd lost them. Selfish bastard, she thought. Should she mention how much she had just paid for a cab to get home? No. She chose instead to aim low. "Endanger your hair you mean."

Indeed, Hector spent thousands of dollars of their income on hair implants, teeth caps, cosmetic surgery, barbers, personal trainers, and cologne.

"What?! What did you say to me?! You don't talk to me like

161

that. You. Do. Not. Talk. To me. Like that."

"Lemme 'lone."

"Junie. We have to talk. Have you seen these?" he said. On the coffee table, their bills were laid out in neat columns. "I don't mean to sound heartless, but do you have any idea how much your mother's hospice care is costing us?"

"Yes.... No.... Doesn't matter."

"It does matter if you look at these bills. But if you look at these bills, you'll see we're already eighty thousand dollars in debt."

She crumpled into the love seat facing him. "Fuck."

"How about your endorsement deals? How are those going?"

"I-I rarely get those anymore. Stupid Mz. Elite and stupid Diamond Girl scoop up the bes' tons."

"What happened to that Goya commercial you were talking about?"

"They went with L-La Nalgona. She's got a much bigger...bigger profile." She giggled.

"Shit then, what are we going to do? Because these bills aren't going to pay themselves, my dear. Listen, again, not to be heartless, maybe there'll be a little something in your mother's will. Do you know?"

"You fuck!"

"Okay, Junie. It's better if we talk in the morning once you sober up. I'll be in the guest room. Again. And by the way, Dr. Carter called. She says you need to get over there."

Judith Jiminez (aka Lady Lava) looked tiny in the cold, white, refrigerated bed Juniper had recently had custom-installed in her bedroom. This woman who had made a giant lens out of Jones Beach sand, who had incinerated an asteroid that would have wiped out Cleveland, who had heated a city block that had lost power during a blizzard.

When Juniper took her mother's hand, it was almost too hot

for her to hold.

"Mom."

"My sweet, sweet Junie," she in a voice that was shrunken, too. Steam rose from around her eyes. "I missed you."

"I'm sorry, Mom. I—"

"Don't worry, sweetheart. It looks like I almost went supernova! Imagine what would happen then!"

"I don't want to. Dr. Carter says your temperature is coming down slowly. You'll be all right."

"I better be. I just finished writing my cookbook—*Lady Lava's Spicy Cajun Secrets!* It's too bad my agent won't return my calls."

"Maybe he knows you can't cook."

"Like that matters. Look at Diamond Girl. She writes self-help books and she needs more help than anybody!"

They laughed together at his, Judith's laugh a little raspier, a little wheezier than ever.

"So. Tell me," Judith said, "what happened with Aqua-Bella? Want to talk about it?"

"I don't know, Mom. My powers just up and went away."

"Oh that's happened to me plenty of times."

"Really? You never told me."

"It was usually just nerves or something. One time I had no powers for three days because I ate some bad hollandaise."

"But they came back?"

"Sometimes quite suddenly. One time, I hadn't been able to flame on for a week and Gary—you remember Gary—he and I were in bed, and, well, poor man had to get skin grafts."

Juniper laughed. "I've just never felt anything like this before." She leaned on the pillow next to her mother, feeling the heat radiate off of her.

"Let me ask you this, honey," Judith said, stroking her daughter's hair, straightening each curl with each stroke like she used to do when Juniper was a teen. "Are things all right with Hector?"

"Hector is Hector."

163

"Well, crimefighting is tough on a relationship. Look at me." Judith had married the reformed Max Fleischmann, aka, Mr. Suave. He had a radioactively-enhanced knack for playing cards, especially pinochle, and so was rich with money and women, but he'd gotten jealous of Judith's late nights in her skimpy costume. Her second husband—Juniper's father—had no superpowers at all. Bill Jiminez worked as a civil engineer, and Juniper remembered him as a tall, diffident man. One of her mom's lesser villains, The Bird Nerd, had sussed her secret identity and confronted the couple. Fearing for his life, Lady Lava told Bill to leave town. He smiled at that, saying there was no reason a villain would harm him, and, he'd said, "You'd come and rescue me anyway." The next day, while Lady Lava was stopping terrorists across town, Bill was shot and killed. She considered revenge, dismissed it. Anyway, soon after the Bird Nerd was killed by his own mutant canary.

"Oh, Mom. The thing is, I've been thinking about it. I honestly don't feel too bad about being normal. I mean, commuting is a pain. But it's nice, not having to worry about other people's problems, not having to come in and save the day."

"Oh, Junie! Don't you think that's a bit selfish? You're not like everybody else. You have an obligation. You know when I first got these powers, I didn't want them. I mean, of all the powers for a Latina! You know, I stopped that volcano from erupting, and the next day, what do the newspapers call me? 'Spitfire!'"

"I remember. You told me."

"Well, I wasn't going to be their 'Spitfire.' Even though, yes, I could literally spit fire. So I had a press conference. I named myself. 'Lady Lava.' But once I did that I couldn't back down. I made a stand. I built a legend, sweetheart, and you were born part of it. Face it. We're heroes. We're role models. And after I sizzle away, it's up to you to keep it going."

"Please don't say that. Don't talk about that."

"I was a lot of things, sweetie—the Blazing Beauty, the

Wildfire Woman, the Countess of Conflagration—but I'm no eternal flame. You need to get used to that."

That night, Juniper found herself at Tim Riley's Bar & Grille again. At the same table as before Roger was staring with adoration at Bella, who reflected the dark liquid in the bottom of her glass.

"Sam!" she said when Juniper approached the table. "It's great to see you!"

They hugged. She didn't know why, but she was happy to see her.

"Sit down and have a drink," Bella said.

"Good times. Tickly drinks," Roger said.

Three rounds in, Bella said, "Now, Sam. I don't think you told us: What do you do for a living, sweetheart?"

"Me? Um, schoolteacher."

"No supplies," said Roger. "No respect."

"Of course!" Bella said. "Pretty and smart and understanding as you are. With a little fetish for the super-life."

"Me? What? No."

"Darling, what else would you be doing here? It can't be the atmosphere."

"But I—"

"Don't worry. It's not like you're married, are you? Doesn't matter. Not our business. But Roger and I have been talking. We like you," said Bella. "We really like you."

"Then I like her, too," said a deep voice, someone suddenly standing by the table. It was Javier. Finally.

He was in costume: a shiny green leotard with an X across the chest, large, bulbous shades, and a pair of transparent wings. The LatinX Fly (formerly the Latin@ Fly, formerly the Latino Fly, formerly the Hispanic Fly, formerly the Latin Fly, formerly the Spanish Fly, all of which made him older than he looked). Considered an antihero, quick to switch sides (every kind of side), he was said to be able to seduce anyone, anything. He greeted Bella with a quick kiss on each cheek, and then he kissed Juniper slowly on both checks. He had a perfectly sculpted mustache and beard, and his breath smelled of pizza and cigarettes.

"Of course, you're not going to let me dance alone?" he said to Juniper.

Aqua-Bella told her: "You better watch out for Javier, sweetheart. He's been the ruin of many a good girl."

Javier was already lifting her from her seat and leading her to the dance floor. The jukebox played a cheesy '80s rock ballad Juniper used to hate but found herself suddenly loving. He spun her around and the world sparkled with joy and color and freedom.

On the dance floor, Javier held her close, crushing their crotches together and firmly grabbing her rear end. "What are you doing here? And with your archenemy. You came looking for me, didn't you, baby?"

Juniper giggled—half at his lines, but half at the attention. The Fly smelled good, damned good. She knew in the back of her mind that he might be using a chemical aphrodisiac but she didn't care. All she could think about was bouncing on his thick muscular thighs.

Ten minutes later they were in the back alley behind the bar. His goggles had flown off and she could see his perfectly sculpted eyebrows.

She felt dirty, she felt alive, she felt on fire—and not in the ten-thousand-degree La Volcana way, but better. Better.

Juniper was trying to find a cab, her head still buzzing, when Hector pulled up in his car in front of her.

"I thought I'd save you the cab fare."

Surprised, embarrassed, wasted, she silently slumped into the car.

166

"Seatbelt," Hector said.

She watched the buildings go by, the signposts on the expressway. She wiped away tears and snot from her face.

"You know it's too bad you're not a supervillain," Hector said. "We could be living the good life."

"I'm sure it's not as easy as you think," she managed to say.

"I don't know, I'm not a supervillain. I'm not super-anything..."

She groaned, waiting for the old joke.

"...except super-handsome. But you, you're really super. Maybe that's why you're hanging out with those new friends of yours. What? You don't think it's easy to keep track of you? Don't worry. You know me, I'm not the jealous type. But once I found out about them, about all of them, I said to myself, 'Self, maybe Junie's planning something. Maybe she has been thinking about our bills. And if she's found a way to make our bills go away, you have to support her one hundred percent.'"

She turned to face him, and her voice gurgled in her throat. "You're crazy. First of all, how dare you fucking spy on me? Second, I'm not planning anything. I'm just having fun, for the first time in a long time. For the first time in a long time, I feel like myself!"

He stopped the car in front of a motel. A blinking sign read, "La Vista Inn: We now have wifi!" He turned and got a duffle bag from the backseat.

"How nice for you. I appreciate your calmly explaining that to me. It's better than our first fight, when you burned a Mohawk on me, remember? By the way, you're staying here tonight. And for the duration. Not because I'm jealous, of course, but because you need to solidify your cover."

"What cover? What are you—"

"Here's the way it will go. You find out when Aqua-Bella's next job is. You tag along with her and her crew, sign up, become a Bell, get a uniform, whole works. And when they've got their backs turned, you take it all from them. And like that, all our troubles are done and forgotten."

"Hector. First of all, don't you listen? My powers—"

"—are gone. Yeah, I heard you. But you're a smart girl. You'll figure it out. And—before you open your mouth again—you'll do it because I can be on the news in a minute with pictures of you and that Fly guy humping like dogs in the alley. It'll break your mother's heart and destroy her legacy and any legacy you were planning. So sleep well, sweetheart! Don't let the bed bugs bite. Because that's what the reviews say about this place. Tomorrow you start your new career!"

Juniper stayed in the motel room, which wasn't that bad. There was hot water, and the bed was comfy and bug free. For the first few days, she was hiccup-crying, convulsing-crying, drooling-crying, and then she realized that of course Javier had just been using her, had used his mojo on her and of course she had become addicted. She had been going through withdrawal. She slept, ate junk food, watched TV, let her nails become horrible to look at.

At the end of the week, she still felt shaky as she walked back to a convenience store to buy more cookies, *chifles*, and Coco Rico than she would have ever allowed herself as La Volcana.

Right outside of the store was a little girl, about ten years old, sitting on a concrete parking bumper, with her head on her folded arms across her knees. Even though the girl was folded in half, it was easy to see what she was wearing.

"Is that a La Volcana costume?" Juniper said, sitting down next to her.

"Uh huh," the girl said, not lifting her head.

"Are you sad about something?"

"Mommy said she wasn't going to get me candy because I was lazy."

"Lazy?"

"I didn't clean the clothes."

"Your mother sounds like my husband. Actually, she sounds

like my mother. My mother used to make me work very hard. I had to practice every day, all the time. I couldn't date, couldn't go to parties. Discipline and obligation and control, that was all that mattered. But that didn't make me happy. I can see that now."

"My mommy hits me."

"My mother said if I didn't listen to her she would rain enough fire down on me to turn me into smoke."

The little girl raised her head and blinked at her. "Whaaat?"

"Um, anyway, sometimes it's important to do things on your own, for yourself. To find your own path."

"Uh huh."

Juniper got up, ready to go back in the store and get the girl some candy. She said, "So, you like La Volcana, huh?"

"Not really. My Diamond Girl costume is dirty."

"That's too bad, kid," she said and went back to the motel.

In her room, Juniper called her mother to see how she was doing, to have a good talk with Lady Lava about the future of La Volcana. Dr. Carter answered the phone and told her to come right away. Her mother had fallen into a coma.

Jupiter rushed to her mother's house. A fully-equipped hospital would've been better, but her mother insisted on maintaining her secret identity until the end.

As Juniper looked on, her mother had a massive seizure that melted the refrigerated bed to the concrete floor. By the time it was over, Judith Jiminez was dead of heart failure.

Months before, Juniper had visited her mother, flying down through a human-sized chimney. Judith's home was decorated with trophies and souvenirs and smelled of lavender and burned toast.

When Juniper had walked in, she found her mother in her usual spot, reclining on her fire-engine red chaise lounge. Judith chatted on the phone, watched TV, and tossed frozen bon-bons into her mouth, where they would disintegrate upon her tongue.

Which was why she said it was fine for her to eat so many, against doctor's orders.

"Happy birthday, Mom. Here, I got you this," Juniper said, pulling a box out of a shopping bag.

Judith unwrapped the present: a vase shaped like a flame. "This is beautiful! What is it?"

"A vase. I fired it myself. It's for your bathroom."

"I'll love looking at it when I poo!" Judith said. "But, say, this would make a great urn."

"Don't say that."

"When the time comes, I want to be cremated, I want you to do it."

"What?! Mom, that is sick, so sick! I can't believe you'd ask me to do that."

"Just listen to your mother. It would be beautiful, it's who we are, and it's what I want. Be a good girl, be a good superhero, and do what your mother says."

"Okay, Mom. I'll do it. So sick."

But when the time came, Juniper couldn't do it. The casket was wheeled up to a dark opening in a wall and fed in. Juniper walked to an interior room. The casket stood on a gurney, dull and silent. Juniper put her hands on the cold surface of the casket and concentrated. Nothing happened. She pulled her hands away and saw her palms had left moisture on the lid that quickly evaporated.

She turned and there was Nikki and she crumpled into her arms.

"It's okay, girl," Nikki said, "let it go."

Behind Nikki, Juniper saw Hector, his hair recently frosted. He came up to them, and Nikki surrendered Juniper to her.

As he hugged her, he whispered, "Do you have any idea how much this funeral is going to cost? You better hurry."

"I do this, Hector, and that's it. You'll have nothing on me, and you get out of my life."

"Whatever you like. But get that money, honey."

* * *

"Where's Roger?" Juniper said.

The archvillainess was tinted and small—clearly drunk—sitting at her table. "Casing our next set-up. Sit down! We haven't seen you in a while. You look th—" Bella starting coughing, sending waves and waves through her body.

"You okay? Can I get you some water?"

Aqua-Bella threw back her head—so fast that droplets landed on the wall behind her—and laughed. "Oh, Sam, you are funny."

"Sorry. I didn't know what—"

"I'm fine. Fine! Hey, you missed the big news. Roger and I are planning a big score. It's going to be big! And we talked it over: We think you could be a Diving Bell. And this is a chance to get your feet wet." She laughed and coughed at that.

Juniper patted her back, watching the ripples they made. "I'm—I'm not sure."

"Not sure? Hon, I can see something's troubling you. It's all over your face. And you didn't drag yourself back to a place like this for no reason. You're looking for something, something dangerous. Well, take it from an old lady: You have an obligation to yourself to be happy, don't you think? Don't you deserve to be happy?"

Juniper didn't know why she was hesitating. This was all she needed. Aqua-Bella was making it easy for her. Do this, and she could dump Hector, forget La Volcana and her legacy, and get on with her life.

"Yes." Juniper smiled. "Yes."

"Hurray! You're in the gang!"

"I can't—I can't think of anything I want more."

Roger showed up soon in a loud shirt with fish sticks on it. He kissed Juniper on the check and then went around and wedged in next to Bella.

"All set," he set. "Three days from today."

"You think it'll go easy?" Bella said.

"As an easy chair," Roger said. "As an ocean breeze."

"Good. We just need to keep clear of La Volcana."

At the mention of her name, Juniper felt her stomach turn.

"Not to worry," Roger said, waving for the bartender. "Seems like she's on vacation."

"I'll tell you who could use a vacation," Bella said. "I could use a vacation, that's who."

"Sun. Sand. Citrus," Roger said.

"Why don't you?" Juniper said. "Why don't you just...stop? Now, before anything bad happens. Retire. Write a book."

"Hah! That's exactly why we need this caper. When we get this, we'll have enough to get out of this crummy business. I mean, Roger and I are no spring chickens."

"You are an ever-running spring," he said.

"Charmer," Bella said to him. "I'll tell you where I want to retire to. Somewhere tropical, where there's an immense ocean, and I'll have one last cigarette and one last drink, and then wade in, melt in to the big, blue ocean, and sayonara."

"Endless water. Into the infinite," Roger said.

"Don't say that. That's not funny."

"Sam, take it easy," Bella said. "I was just talking."

"I'm okay," she said, downing her vodka tonic and signaling for another. "Let's...let's talk about the caper. What can I do?"

Three days later, at 9 a.m., at the corner of 57th and 5th, Aqua-Bella and her matching, hooded Bells jumped out of the Aqua Van and filed into Darwish's Jewelry Exchange. Roger waited in the van, nervously tapping the steering wheel.

As the workers looked up, Aqua-Bella nodded to Juniper Jiminez.

"Mesdames and messieurs," Juniper said through her mask, "Please welcome...Aqua-Bella and her Diving Bells!"

Bella winked at her and took center stage, "Good morning all and welcome to a wonderful robbery! Before you do anything, please be aware that I have already kiboshed all of your surveillance equipment as well as all of your phones. You'll have to get new ones, sorry, my dears, but think of the stories you'll have to tell and posts you'll be able to post after this. You'll get so many Likes! Now if you'll all cooperate, we'll all be able to go back to our morning lattes and enjoy the lovely summer day."

The jewelry store workers were instructed to toss money and wallets and jewelry into the sacks that Juniper Jiminez and the four other Bells held open. Juniper was filled with shame, not just for what she was doing, but also for what she planned to do later: somehow, as soon as she found an opportunity, hijack the van and bring the loot to Hector. It would all be over quickly, she told herself, and she could finally live the life she wanted.

"So where are you from?" Bella asked the manager.

"Albuquerque," he mumbled.

"Albuquerque! How nice! I hear it's so hot in Albuquerque, the chickens lay hard-boiled eggs! That's a lovely tie, sir! How about you, young lady?"

As Bella went from person to person, the sack Juniper held got heavier. Everything was going smoothly—until a piercing banshee song crashed through the front doors of the store.

It was Sonic Sistah. With a voice that boomed like a diety, she said, "Put the bags down and your hands up!"

Juniper's heart beat wildly. How was she going to explain this?

She turned and saw all the water in the store, all the liquid that had been clogging the cameras and alarms and phones, suck back into Aqua-Bella, who with a wave from her hand sent a fountain of water right into Sonic Sistah's mouth, knocking her down and encasing her. Nikki struggled to get up, but the water overwhelmed her.

Juniper cried out: "You're killing her!'"

"I can't be stopped this time. No more screw-ups! No more cheap hauls!"

Sonic Sista held her hands to her throat. She was drowning.

"Stop!" Juniper held her hand up—heat began to rise, from

173

the core through her chest, and rocketing up her arm and out of her palm shot a flame, and it hit Bella dead on, sizzling.

Bella looked at Juniper, surprised, betrayed.

The flame continued to shoot from La Volcana's hand. Bella began to steam, which would have been enough to weaken her, to make her give up. But Juniper was unable to stop the flame flowing from her.

"Oh no," she whispered. "Not like this." Her power had come back, uncorked and unstoppable. If she moved the flow of fire away from Bella, it would kill anyone else in the store. The only person she could focus on, the only person who could possibly withstand it was Bella.

The archvillain's body began to shrink, and soon she could no longer control any of her molecules. She wasn't just turning to steam. Every part of her was disintegrating. Her eyes saddened—but then as she began to disappear, her mouth opened to laugh. But there was no sound. And then she was gone.

And suddenly as it came out, Juniper's first burst ceased, and the air in the store was dry and crisp.

"Bella! My Bella!" It was Roger. He turned to her. "What have you done?"

Sonic Sistah knocked him out with a high C. She rushed over to Juniper Jiminez. "Junie, I knew it was you."

She nodded. "I—"

"Please. Thank *you* for saving me. I'm so sorry I busted in. I didn't know you were doing undercover work. Great idea!"

"But—"

"Your mother would be so proud."

Sonic Sistah took Juniper's hand and raised it in the air and in a voice that echoed for miles, that was recorded and downloaded and commented on and even earned a trending hashtag, she said, "All hail La Volcana, superhero of the day. Superhero of the city! Superhero forever!"

Under her Bell hood, tears as hot as a star streamed down Juniper's face.

SOUTHSIDE VALENTINE

Detective Almodovar, half Polish, half Puerto Rican, sits in the playground at the corner of Borinquen Plaza and Rodney Street. Snow dandruffs the monkey bars, but except for Almodovar it's empty on a February morning. He sits on a metal seat and his ass is as cold as his coffee.

This will be an easy collar, the kind they turn into schlocky *20/20* episodes. All this woman had to do was say the four magic words: "Please kill my husband."

The park is located at a traffic-busy corner, long chains of vans and cars and semi-trucks heading onto or avoiding the BQE. Diagonally across is a glass and concrete castle for the rich, one of those corpse-looking new construction buildings that scrape against all the good old stuff in the neighborhood, all the good stuff he remembers from when he lived here, just blocks away.

And right across the street is the artsy-fartsy P.S. 414—"Arbor School"—which used to be the great P.S. 19, where he used to daydream about a sweet-faced girl named Brunhilda Rodriguez, who sat in front of him and made his chest swell and his tighty whities tighter.

A half hour passes and Almodovar figures Señora X, as she called herself online, has chickened out, until he sees a woman in flip-flops and trotting straight for him across Rodney Street, from the direction of the tenements that still line South 3rd. She takes a seat across from him at a concrete checkerboard table.

She says, "You him? I gotta get back upstairs in fifteen minutes. I got food on the stove. This is crazy." She smells of cilantro and milk and *ajo* and menthol but right away he sees it's Brunhilda, twenty years older but what other Latina in Los Sures has such freckles starred across a flat button nose, such golden eyes, such red-brown waves. No one that he ever cared to see. Something was mixed in her, which he loved because that made her just like him.

As she lights a cigarette and looks around, distrustful, he wonders at the curves under the oversized hoodie. He's moved on in his heart, of course. What does your heart know when you're twelve years old? He's married now and has three boys all practicing to be MMA fighters on the furniture and each other's heads.

"Shit, it's cold," she says, then she goes through the expected litany. *The husband cheats. Beats the kids. Disrespects her family. Doesn't work. Drinks too much. Kicks the chihuahua.*

"It's Valentine's Day," she says, "and I know where he's going to be from 6 o'clock to 9 o'clock. I know where his girl-friend lives, so all you have to do is wait for him there."

And what? She has to say it, so he can pull out the cuffs and call in the officers laced all around the park.

He looks at her eyes, and he thinks maybe there is recognition there. But why would she remember him, the stuttering little geeky crusher who sat behind her for three grades? He'd filled out, a lot, and was free of the mop of hair he insisted in hiding behind.

She reaches into her hoodie and he sees a fat envelope and he knows this is it when they hear "Bitch! Who is this motherfucker now? I knew it! I knew it!"

A man in a parka stands across the street, pointing at Almodovar and yelling at her. The man steps off the curb at a run,

176

not even looking.

Almodovar remembers later, in the report he writes up, that the van was one of those prepared meal kit delivery vans you see all over the neighborhood now.

The woman's husband bounces off the front of the van and twenty feet away his body gets wrapped around a fire hydrant.

There is a pause.

Almodovar stands up to do something, he's not sure what. He turns to the woman, who is zipping up her hoodie, attempting to erase the existence of the envelope. He could still bring her in, could still make trouble for her.

For a moment she looks at him and smiles a quick smile, or is it a plea for mercy? He can't quite read it. Then the moment is gone.

"Never mind, mister," she mumbles, already turning. Then she runs, screaming her husband's name. "You're not going to visit that bitch tonight now. Shit, and I still got rice on the stove."

Almodovar hears chatter on his earpiece, and he knows someone has already called for an ambulance.

Before he throws out his empty coffee cup, he makes a mental note to remember to pick up flowers for Migdalia and to get a new game for the boys to keep them busy.

ACKNOWLEDGMENTS

"La Volcana" first appeared as "Volcano Girl" in *A Thousand Faces* (November 2010); "Old Pendejo" first appeared in *Tales of the Zombie War* (July 2010); "Good Fences" first appeared in *Powder Burn Flash* (May 2011); "Meet Me at the Clock" first appeared in *Grand Central Noir* (June 2013); "How to Kill a Brown Girl (Or Black, White, or Halfsie)" first appeared in *Shotgun Honey* (March 2014); "Pale Yellow Sun" first appeared in *Sunshine Noir* (September 2016); "Merry Xmas from Orchard Beach" first appeared in *Spinetingler* (December 2016); "Southside Valentine" first appeared as part of Akashic Books Mondays Are Murder series (February 2019); "Withhold the Dawn" first appeared in *Tiny Crimes: Very Short Tales of Mystery and Murder* (June 2018); "Bobo" first appeared in *Pa'que Tu Lo Sepas! Stories to Benefit the People of Puerto Rico* (October 2019); "Blackout" first appeared in *Mystery Tribune* (Nov./Dec. 2019).

Big thanks to all the editors and publishers who gave these stories homes. Those of you who read them when they were originally published may note many differences from their original forms. That's because I am one of those writers who cannot leave well enough alone. In deciding to put this volume together, I knew I wanted to revise. So I took an unusual step (for me) and sent one to two pieces to friends and fellow authors whose work

ACKNOWLEDGMENTS

I respect and I asked them for feedback. Having their extra eyes on these stories proved invaluable, and not only did their insight improve the work, but also in several cases they helped me come up with much better endings. So, deep, sincere, tremendous thanks to Peter R. Emshwiller, Graham Everett, Juliet Fletcher, Matthew David Goodwin, Jennifer Kitses, Dustin Michael, Erica Obey, and Radha Vatsal. Thanks to the Down & Out team of Eric Campbell and Lance Wright. And thanks as always to my wife Denise for her love and support.

Richie Narvaez is the author of *Hipster Death Rattle, Holly Hernandez and the Death of Disco,* and *Roachkiller and Other Stories,* which won the Spinetingler Award for Best Anthology/Short Story Collection. His work has appeared in *Ellery Queen Mystery Magazine, Latinx Rising: An Anthology of Science Fiction and Fantasy, Indian Country Noir, Mississippi Review, Pilgrimage,* and *Tiny Crimes: Very Short Tales of Mystery and Murder,* among others. He served as president of the Mystery Writers of America, New York Chapter, as Bronx Council on the Arts Artist in Residence, and as a judge for the 2019 PEN America's Open Book Awards. He teaches at the Fashion Institute of Technology in Manhattan and lives in the Bronx.

BOOKS

On the following pages are a few
more great titles from the
Down & Out Books publishing family.

For a complete list of books and to
sign up for our newsletter,
go to DownAndOutBooks.com.

Rattlesnake Rodeo
A Boise Longpig Hunting Club Thriller
Nick Kolakowski

Down & Out Books
October 2020
978-1-64396-128-6

The fiery sequel to *Boise Longpig Hunting Club* is here…

Jake Halligan and his ultra-lethal sister Frankie have survived the Boise Longpig Hunting Club. What comes next, though, might prove far worse.

With the law closing in, they'll have to make the hardest choices if they want to survive.

Below the Line
Steven Jankowski

Down & Out Books
November 2020
978-1-64396-154-5

Between gigs as a Hollywood movie Teamster, Mike Millek freelances as an armed chauffeur to the stars.

When Mike arrives one night to pick up his successful but deadbeat rap producer client, whom he finds freshly murdered with a satchel full of cash, Mike decides to take what is owed him, leading him down a path into the sordid underbelly of the Hollywood power elite.

Blood by Choice
Rob Pierce

All Due Respect, an imprint of
Down & Out Books
September 2020
978-1-64396-116-3

Two women and a child are murdered. Dust, who unknowingly set them up, returns to Berkeley to find the killer. With his old buddy Karma in tow, Dust discovers that one of the culprits was Vollmer, a ruthless hired gun working for Dust's former boss, Rico. When Vollmer finds out Dust is in town the hunt becomes mutual.

In this, the third book of the Uncle Dust series, old debts are paid and new ones incurred. Brutish, dangerous men lurk in every corner and slaughter runs rampant.

Shotgun Honey Presents Volume 4: RECOIL
Ron Earl Phillips, editor

Shotgun Honey, an imprint of
Down & Out Books
May 2020
978-1-64396-138-5

With new and established authors from around the world, Shotgun Honey Presents Volume 4: RECOIL delivers stories that explore a darker side of remorse, revenge, circumstance, and humanity.

Contributors: Rusty Barnes, Susan Benson, Sarah M. Chen, Kristy Claxton, Jen Conley, Brandon Daily, Barbara DeMarco-Barrett, Hector Duarte Jr., Danny Gardner, Tia Ja'nae, Carmen Jaramillo, Nick Kolakowski, JJ Landry, Bethany Maines, Tess Makovesky, Alexander Nachaj, David Nemeth, Cindy O'Quinn, Brandon Sears, Johnny Shaw, Kieran Shea, Gigi Vernon, Patrick Whitehurst.

CPSIA information can be obtained
at www.ICGtesting.com
Printed in the USA
LVHW030338111121
702982LV00006B/1119